# HALL OF FAME
*Rangers' All-Time Greats*

BOB MACCALLUM

# HALL OF FAME
## *Rangers' All-Time Greats*

First published in Great Britain in 2009 by The Breedon Books Publishing Company Limited, Breedon House, 3 The Parker Centre, Derby, DE21 4SZ

This paperback edition published in Great Britain in 2014 by DB Publishing, an imprint of JMD Media Ltd

## Acknowledgements

Many thanks to Robert McKee and Action Images for supplying photographs used in this book.

## Dedication

To my wife Jessica, for everything.

ISBN 978-1-78091-391-9

Printed and bound in the UK by Copytech (UK) Ltd Peterborough

# Contents

# HALL OF FAM

| | |
|---|---|
| 1872 - 1882 | MOSES McNEIL |
| 1874 - 1884 | TOM VALLANCE |
| 1891 - 1903 | JOHN McPHERSON |
| 1893 - 1905 | NICOL SMITH |
| 1894 - 1915 | ALEX SMITH |
| 1907 - 1920 | JIMMY GORDON |
| 1913 - 1927 | TOMMY CAIRNS |
| 1914 - 1929 | ANDY CUNNINGHAM |
| 1915 - 1927 | BERT MANDERSON |
| 1917 - 1930 | TOMMY MUIRHEAD |
| 1917 - 1934 | SANDY ARCHIBALD |
| 1920 - 1933 | ALAN MORTON |
| 1920 - 1936 | DAVID MEIKLEJOHN |
| 1925 - 1945 | DOUGIE GRAY |
| 1927 - 1940 | BOB McPHAIL |
| 1930 - 1946 | JIMMY SMITH |
| 1931 - 1945 | JERRY DAWSON |

| | |
|---|---|
| 1933 - 1946 | ALEX VENTORS |
| 1937 - 1954 | WILLIE THORNTON |
| 1938 - 1953 | JOCK SHAW |
| 1938 - 1956 | WILLIE WOODBURN |
| 1938 - 1956 | WILLIE WADDELL |
| 1939 - 1950 | TORRY GILLICK |
| 1941 - 1957 | GEORGE YOUNG |
| 1945 - 1961 | IAN McCOLL |
| 1946 - 1955 | SAMMY COX |
| 1946 - 1956 | BOBBY BROWN |
| 1949 - 1959 | JOHNNY HUBBARD |
| 1950 - 1959 | BILLY SIMPSON |
| 1952 - 1966 | ERIC CALDOW |
| 1952 - 1965 | RALPH BRAND |
| 1954 - 1963 | ALEX SCOTT |
| 1955 - 1967 | BILLY RITCHIE |
| 1955 - 1967 | JIMMY MILLAR |

| | | |
|---|---|---|
| 1956 - 1964 | BOBBY SHEARER | 1971 |
| 1956 - 1967 | DAVIE WILSON | 1972 |
| 1958 - 1970 | DAVIE PROVAN | 1977 |
| 1960 - 1965 | JIM BAXTER | 1977 |
| 1960 - 1973 | RONNIE McKINNON | 1983 |
| 1961 - 1972 | WILLIE HENDERSON | 1984 |
| 1961 - 1978 | JOHN GREIG | 1986 |
| 1962 - 1975 | WILLIE MATHIESON | 1986 |
| 1963 - 1982 | COLIN JACKSON | 1986 |
| 1964 - 1972 | WILLIE JOHNSTON | 1987 |
| 1964 - 1982 | SANDY JARDINE | 1987 |
| 1966 - 1974 | DAVE SMITH | 1988 |
| 1968 - 1972 | COLIN STEIN | 1988 |
| 1968 - 1974 | ALFIE CONN | 1990 |
| 1968 - 1981 | ALEX MacDONALD | 1991 |
| 1968 - 1983 | DEREK JOHNSTONE | 1991 |
| 1970 - 1986 | PETER McCLOY | 1994 |

MMY McLEAN
M FORSYTH
BBY RUSSELL
VIE COOPER
LY McCOIST
I DURRANT
RRY BUTCHER
AEME SOUNESS
RIS WOODS
Y WILKINS
CHARD GOUGH
HN BROWN
N FERGUSON
ARK HATELEY
UART McCALL
DY GORAM
IAN LAUDRUP

1995 - 1998    PAUL GASCOIGNE
1996 - 2001    JORG ALBERTZ
1996 - 2003    BARRY FERGUSON

# Introduction

Each chapter of this book, which is arranged in chronological order, gives a summary of the period in which the players elected to the Rangers' Hall of Fame played. Also described are the managers who signed those players. Some players with longer careers at Ibrox, such as Ally McCoist, played under more than one manager. He, in fact, played under four Rangers managers. That is why in this book the Hall of Fame players are arranged under the manager who signed them and appear in the order in which they joined the club.

## Rangers' Hall of Fame

Rangers' Hall of Fame was set up by Sir David Murray in 2000 as a way of honouring some of the legendary players who helped make the club the success it is today. Five criteria are applied to candidates, and the fans vote each year on the nominees from each decade from the 1950s onwards, originally electing two from each era. The initial list, which contained players from the earliest days of the club, was compiled by a committee consisting of Sir David Murray, John Greig, Sandy Jardine, club historian David Mason and Ally McCoist. Currently, 74 stars have had their names picked out in gold lettering on the Hall of Fame panel above the famed marble staircase inside Ibrox.

## The criteria for nomination are:

*Service to the club
*Number of games
*Honours won
*International caps
*Exceptional ability

# Roll of Honour

## Elected Players 1872–1920 (Manager: William Wilton)

| | |
|---|---|
| Moses McNeil | 1872–82 |
| Tom Vallance | 1874–84 |
| John McPherson | 1891–1902 |
| Nicol Smith | 1893–1905 |
| Alec Smith | 1894–1915 |
| Jimmy Gordon | 1907–20 |
| Tommy Cairns | 1913–27 |
| Andy Cunningham | 1914–29 |
| Bert Manderson | 1915–27 |
| Tommy Muirhead | 1917–30 |
| Sandy Archibald | 1917–34 |
| David Meiklejohn | 1919–36 |

The Hall of Fame panel situated above the famous marble staircase inside Ibrox.

## Elected Players 1920–54 (Manager: Bill Struth)

| | |
|---|---|
| Alan Morton | 1920–33 |
| Dougie Gray | 1925–47 |
| Bob McPhail | 1927–40 |
| Jimmy Smith | 1928–46 |
| Sam English | 1931–33 |
| Jerry Dawson | 1931–45 |
| Torry Gillick | 1933–35 & 1946–50 |
| Alex Venters | 1933–46 |
| Willie Thornton | 1936–54 |
| Willie Waddell | 1936–55 |
| Jock Shaw | 1938–53 |
| Willie Woodburn | 1938–54 |
| George Young | 1941–57 |
| Ian McColl | 1945–60 |
| Sammy Cox | 1946–55 |
| Bobby Brown | 1946–56 |

Two great wingers who spanned the generations: Willie Waddell and Davie Cooper, as shown on a panel in the Blue Room at Ibrox.

Some famous Rangers captains, from Tom Vallance to Lorenzo Amoruso, as shown on a panel in the Blue Room at Ibrox.

| | |
|---|---|
| Johnny Hubbard | 1949–59 |
| Billy Simpson | 1950–59 |
| Eric Caldow | 1953–66 |
| Ralph Brand | 1954–65 |
| Alex Scott | 1954–63 |

## Elected Players 1954–67 (Manager: Scot Symon)

| | |
|---|---|
| Billy Ritchie | 1955–67 |
| Bobby Shearer | 1955–65 |
| Jimmy Millar | 1955–67 |
| Harold Davis | 1956–64 |
| Davie Wilson | 1956–67 |
| Davie Provan | 1958–70 |
| Willie Henderson | 1960–72 |
| Ronnie McKinnon | 1960–73 |
| Willie Mathieson | 1960–75 |

Barry Ferguson, as shown on a panel in the Blue Room at Ibrox.

| | |
|---|---|
| Jim Baxter | 1960–65 & 1969–70 |
| John Greig | 1961–78 |
| Colin Jackson | 1963–82 |
| Sandy Jardine | 1964–82 |
| Willie Johnston | 1964–72 & 1980–82 |
| Dave Smith | 1966–74 |

## Elected Players 1967–69 (Manager: Davie White)

| | |
|---|---|
| Alfie Conn | 1968–74 |
| Colin Stein | 1968–73 & 1975–77 |
| Alex McDonald | 1968–80 |

## Elected Players 1969–72 (Manager: Willie Waddell)

| | |
|---|---|
| Derek Johnstone | 1970–83 & 1985–86 |
| Peter McCloy | 1970–86 |
| Tommy McLean | 1971–82 |

## Elected Players 1972–78 (Manager: Jock Wallace)

| | |
|---|---|
| Tom Forsyth | 1972–82 |
| Davie Cooper | 1977–89 |
| Bobby Russell | 1977–86 |

## Elected Players 1983–86 (Manager: John Greig)

| | |
|---|---|
| Ally McCoist | 1983–98 |
| Ian Durrant | 1983–98 |

## Elected Players 1986–91 (Manager: Graeme Souness)

| | |
|---|---|
| Graeme Souness | 1986–91 |
| Terry Butcher | 1986–90 |
| Chris Woods | 1986–91 |

The Rangers mosaic crest at the main entrance to Ibrox Stadium.

Rangers managers, from William Wilton to Dick Advocaat, as shown on a panel in the Blue Room at Ibrox.

| | |
|---|---|
| Richard Gough | 1987–97 & 1997–98 |
| Ray Wilkins | 1987–89 |
| Ian Ferguson | 1988–2000 |
| John Brown | 1988–97 |
| Mark Hateley | 1990–95 & 97 |

## Elected Players 1991–98 (Manager: Walter Smith)

| | |
|---|---|
| Andy Goram | 1991–98 |
| Stuart McCall | 1991–98 |
| Brian Laudrup | 1994–98 |
| Paul Gascoigne | 1995–98 |
| Jorg Albertz | 1996–2001 |
| Barry Ferguson | 1996–2003 & 2005–2009 |

## Elected Players 1998 –2001 (Manager: Dick Advocaat)

| | |
|---|---|
| Stefan Klos | 1998–2007 |

*Chapter One*

# Players Elected
# Between 1872–1920

## History of the Period

The four youngsters who formed Rangers, although all students in Glasgow, were actually from villages along the Gareloch in Dunbartonshire. Their names were Peter and Moses McNeil, Peter Campbell and William McBeath. Dedicated rowers, they followed their pursuit on the River Clyde as it meandered through Glasgow; however, their sporting enthusiasm was to be channelled in another direction in 1872 thanks to the proximity of Fleshers' Haugh, on Glasgow Green, to the River Clyde. It was this area of the Green that had become reserved for teams playing the relatively new sport of Association football. The founders were all fit youngsters, under 20, with Moses being the youngest at only 16 years of age. Moses is the only founder to make it into the club Hall of Fame. Perhaps this is something that should now be rectified.

The decade before Rangers' foundation had seen the formation of the Football Association in England, and since then the popularity of the new sport had been growing apace, with clubs springing up all over Britain. In Scotland, since 1867, Queen's Park had established itself as the dominant force north of the border. In fact, the four 'boys' who founded Rangers had watched Queen's Park play and had been mightily impressed. This, in conjunction with watching other sides such as Eastern play on Fleshers' Haugh, inspired them to form their own club in February 1872. Moses McNeil proposed that 'The Rangers' be the name of the new club – it was the name of an English rugby club that he had come across, and the impressionable youth just liked the sound of it!

Having found a name, the next step was to find a team. So, teammates had to be recruited to the cause. Naturally, family and friends seemed the obvious solution. Peter Campbell's brother, John, and the McNeils' older brother, William, were enlisted along with others who were mainly teenagers. Indeed, William's career as a fledgling Ranger can be attributed solely to his possession of a football. Apparently, when looking for players for their new club some of the teenage founders thought that William was already 'too old' to become a member; however, through a family work connection, a Mr McDonald from a company based in Buchanan Street had donated a football to William. So, when he was rejected, maybe for the first (but not last) time was heard the expression 'It's ma baw'. William McNeil's attitude was that it was his ball, so if he was not going to get a game the others could find their own ball.

Despite this slight problem, the club was formed and a subscription was taken among the members to accrue the necessary funds. An amicable solution to the dispute over William McNeil's membership must have been found as eventually he proudly took his place in the Gers' first-ever line up.

So, it was in 1873 that The Rangers became a 'proper' club. The first general meeting of the club was held that year, with office bearers elected and all aspects of the club from training to regular fixtures arranged in a more organised fashion. Still, it was the enthusiasm and love for the game of the McNeil brothers, Peter Campbell and Tom Vallance that provided the drive for Rangers throughout those early years.

In March 1873, eight clubs met in a Glasgow hotel to constitute the Scottish Football Association. Unfortunately, the newly formed Rangers club was too late to apply for membership and thus missed competing in the inaugural Scottish Cup, won, predictably, by Queen's Park. Ironically 100 years later Rangers won the centenary Scottish Cup. It must be remembered that, with football in its infancy, the Scottish Cup was the only show in town as there was no other form of competitive football. With Football Leagues not yet having been devised, clubs played each other in a series of 'friendlies', with all their players being amateurs.

What we do know is that the following season, in October 1874, Rangers' first competitive game took place against Oxford in the Scottish Cup, with the Gers winning 2–0, thanks to goals from Moses McNeil and David Gibb.

Rangers only won one trophy in its first 18 years of existence – the Glasgow Merchants' Charity Cup. In fact, it took the club until May 1885 before it recorded its first victory over the aristocrats of the Scottish game, Queen's Park. Before then, Rangers had appeared in two Scottish Cup Finals, losing both in controversial circumstances. The club's first appearance came in the 1876–77 season when Vale of Leven (then approaching Queen's Park in stature) needed three games to beat them. The same side also denied Rangers in the 1878–79 Final.

At the end of March 1890, a delegation of football club administrators met in a Glasgow hotel (hotels seemed to be popular for important meetings in those days) to discuss the setting-up of a Scottish League. Of the 14 established clubs invited, only Queen's Park and Clyde declined to attend. A League was already flourishing in England, so the Scots saw this as the way forward for the game. That inaugural League season of 1890–91 created all sorts of firsts, the main one being Rangers' first League Championship, which the club shared with Dumbarton after 18 matches and a Play-off game. During that first decade of the League Championship, the Ibrox men were not the most dominant: of those 10 Championships, Rangers won three, Celtic managed four, Dumbarton two and Hearts one.

The birth of the 20th century saw the infant Rangers grow into adolescence. Queen Victoria died in January 1901, and with her died the Victorian age. In football terms, Rangers had already left that age behind as it became a more professional and financially successful club, making great strides within the game. In this 20-year spell, Rangers won the League Championship seven times but the Scottish Cup only once. Indeed, this trophy would elude the club in a manner that led many to believe Rangers had a Scottish Cup 'hoodoo'.

As successful in the League as Rangers were, they were still outdone by the club that had already become their greatest rival – Celtic. This period was a golden age for Celtic. Not until the advent of the Jock Stein era in the 1960s would Celtic enjoy such a prolific haul of trophies. In this span of 20 Championships, Celtic finished as champions 11 times and won the Scottish Cup six times, an impressive proportion considering that the Scottish Cup was suspended for the four years of World War One. It was in an article in the sports journal *The Scottish Referee,* in April 1904, that the term 'Old Firm' was first used to describe the relationship of Rangers to Celtic and, indeed, of both clubs to the rest of Scottish football. Few perhaps suspected even then that both clubs would dominate domestic Scottish football, not only over the first 20 years of the new century but for evermore.

The new century had started in the same manner as the previous one had ended – with Rangers as Scottish Champions. Victory in the 1901–02 season had made it four in a row, a success stemming from that great side that had won the title by winning every match. After this run of Rangers success, however, Hibs, Third Lanark and then Celtic on six consecutive occasions prevented Rangers from winning the title again. One of the most significant of Rangers' Championships was undoubtedly the victory in season 1910–11, for this prevented Celtic achieving seven titles in a row and halted, albeit temporarily, Celtic's domination of the Championship. Rangers went on to win three successive titles before Celtic came back at them, winning the next four.

Rangers' performances in the Scottish Cup were also leaving them in Celtic's wake. After winning the trophy in season 1902–03, it was another 25 years before the Scottish Cup was lifted by a Rangers captain. During this period, however, the club did add seven Glasgow Cups and seven Glasgow Charity Cups to its list of honours.

During World War One, the authorities decided that football should continue as normal – or as normal as was possible with many players enlisting to fight in the trenches. As the war dragged on, year after year, the players who had not enlisted to fight had to work in war-related industries. The Old Firm came in for some criticism that not enough of their players had joined the army, but the ones who distinguished themselves in action countered that stance. In addition, William Wilton and Bill Struth did sterling voluntary work at the nearby Bellahouston Hospital, tirelessly working with the wounded soldiers who had been transferred there. Ironically, it was during these war years that players started to join the club who would go on to be the backbone of the brilliant Rangers teams of the 1920s that dominated the League Championship as no other had done before it.

Manager William Wilton and trainer Bill Struth's finest season came in 1919–20, when Rangers won the Championship, losing only two matches out of 42 in the League while scoring 106 goals and conceding only 25. To reinforce just how successful the club had become by then, its average crowd was 30,000 and a record income of £50,946 had been amassed. Then, at the end of the season, tragedy struck when Wilton died in a freak boating accident. Wilton's death stunned all of Scottish football, but Rangers were fortunate that their first manager's successor was already at the club. Struth became manager and so the continuity at the club was not broken, thanks to the fact that Struth had already built relationships with his players and knew exactly how Rangers worked, and he had a clear vision of how it should be in the future. The elevation of Struth to the manager's position signalled the start of the longest period of sustained domination in the history of Scottish football.

## MANAGER: WILLIAM WILTON (1899–1920)

As a youth, William Wilton, a native Glaswegian, was devoted to football and was attracted by the enthusiasm and ambition of Rangers so, in 1883, he paid the required dues to become a member of Rangers Football Club. He was a keen and robust player but did not have enough skill to make the Rangers first XI so had to be content with turning out for the reserves, The Swifts. It soon because obvious to his colleagues that his talent was more for the organisational and administrative side of the game and he soon became The Swifts' match secretary.

In the initial years of the club, it was run by various committees and the post of manager did not exist. Indeed, a 'selecting committee' picked the team for each match and their choice was discussed and ratified (or not) by the 'general

William Wilton.

committee'. Although he was match secretary for The Swifts, Wilton was not a member of the 'selecting committee', but he did contribute to most other aspects of the running of the club and became adept at presenting proposals for progress as well as advocating his case. Such was the status he achieved that, by May 1889, by a large majority of members, he was elected match secretary at the ridiculously young age of 23. It should be said, however, that Rangers at that time was a club whose players and officials were all young so Wilton's age was not a consideration – his appointment was solely based on his undoubted ability as an administrator.

Apart from scheduling Rangers' matches, Wilton's duties extended to most areas of management including the acquisition of new players to develop the side. It was also he who instigated the Rangers Sports and personally supervised the design and construction of the Ibrox running track around the field of play, upon which many records would later be set thanks to its excellence. The Rangers Sports became one of the most important events in the British athletic calendar until the early 1960s.

One of the major tasks Wilton set himself was the extension and improvement of First Ibrox. His plan to build another grandstand to seat 3,000 fans was passed by the club's members, who had come to appreciate his abilities and trust his judgement completely. By the end of the 1880s, most members believed the club to be in a healthy state both on and off the field. With his ever-growing reputation, it became inevitable that, by the end of the next decade, when Rangers became a Limited Liability Company, the man it would elect as its first manager and secretary would be William Wilton. After all, he had been Rangers' manager in all but name prior to this.

Under the guidance of Wilton, Rangers won nine League Championships, five Scottish Cups, 13 Glasgow Cups and 11 Glasgow Charity Cups.

# Players Elected

## Moses McNeil (1872–82)

Moses McNeil was one of seven brothers from a Gareloch family who had moved to Glasgow, and rowing on the Clyde at Glasgow Green was his favourite sport – until he got the football bug. Along with his brother, Peter, Peter Campbell and William McBeath, he founded Rangers and is the one credited with deciding on its name. Since he had been born in 1855, he was only a teenager when he helped to start what was to become Scotland's greatest football club.

In the club's early days the only games that could be played were friendlies and Scottish Cup ties. In the first three seasons of the club's existence, McNeil played in 50 of 52 possible matches. In that first season of 1874–75 he played in all 12 friendly games, scoring three goals, and in Gers' three Scottish Cup games, scoring a goal against Oxford.

McNeil was a small but powerful winger in an era when wingers and attackers in general had to be resilient and brave. He was a tough, dribbling winger who could 'mix it' with opponents when he had to in order to survive. In those days, 'tackling' could be more akin to assault, leaving players really bruised and battered. It was not uncommon for the players, who were amateurs, remember, to have to take time off work to recuperate after a particularly bruising, uncompromising encounter. All that for the love of the game!

McNeil played in Rangers' first two Scottish Cup Finals, unfortunately losing both. The first took place in 1877 when the mighty Vale of Leven took three matches to beat the young Rangers team. McNeil scored the second Gers goal in the third replay, but Vale came from behind to end up 3–2 winners. Even worse, in the 1879 Final Rangers looked like winning, but Vale equalised two minutes from the end. Since Rangers had had a goal disallowed for offside before that, they protested to the SFA, but their protest was dismissed and a replay ordered. A furious Gers refused to turn up for that replay, and the trophy was awarded to Vale. Ironically, a couple of weeks after this, Rangers had to play Vale in the Final of the Glasgow Charity Cup and won 2–1 to collect Gers' only trophy in the first 20 years of its existence. At least the club's founder managed to win a medal before he retired from the game.

In 1876, McNeil was capped for Scotland against Wales, becoming the first Rangers player to play for his country. His last match for Rangers was in April 1882 against Dumbarton in a 2–2 draw in the Charity Cup. When he died in 1938 at the age of 83 he must have been the proudest man in the country to have lived long enough to see the institution that his wee club had become in those 60-odd years since he had named it.

Due to the difficulty caused by the mists of time, an approximate tally of McNeil's career is that he played 107 games and scored 21 goals for Rangers – but it was helping to found the club that was his greatest achievement.

# Tom Vallance (1874–84)

In this era, before Leagues were organised and football was very much in its infancy, legendary players were few and far between. Apart from the founders such as Moses McNeil, perhaps the first great Rangers playing legend was Tom Vallance. Aged 17, young Tom had joined The Rangers in 1873, almost a year after its inception and initial matches. Like the club's founders, he was from Dunbartonshire, and he captained the team for Rangers' first nine seasons.

In a time when people were generally smaller than nowadays, Vallance was considered very tall at 6ft 2in. He may have had a slim build, but he was powerful and, equally important in those early years when football was often a brutal affair, he had a mental toughness about him. He played as a full-back, wearing the number-two jersey for most of his career and taking over the number three at the end of it. He did not miss a match in his first two seasons and missed only three games in his third. A model of consistency with a great spirit, he missed very few matches in total until the 1879–80 season, when he missed half the games played.

Vallance was a talented, all-round athlete, setting a long-jump record as well as being a rower of some repute. He also, unusually, showed an artistic side to his sportsman's nature and had paintings exhibited at the Royal Scottish Academy. Nowadays, fans would be amazed to hear of modern players even visiting an art gallery! At some matches, he could even be seen helping to take the money at the gate (there were no turnstiles then – and no big egos either).

Unfortunately, the two Scottish Cup Finals in which Vallance played were losing affairs, but he did become the only Rangers captain in the club's first 18 years of existence to lift a trophy when Rangers won the Glasgow Merchants' Charity Cup in 1879. The highlights of his career may have been his seven appearances for the Scotland team.

Suffering from a poor season and a Scottish Cup exit just before Vallance's final match against St Mirren, away, in 1882, it was a shame that Rangers had to play with only eight players in a 5–2 defeat. It perhaps showed how low morale had sunk throughout the club. A few days later, Vallance left to take up a position in Calcutta. He was given a fitting send-off by the club at a Glasgow hotel and received 50 sovereigns as a gift. When he boarded the train at Central Station on the first leg of his journey to London, many fans of the club were there to wave farewell.

A year later, however, he was back home suffering from poor health. He joined the club again, but his appearances were limited out of necessity to a few sporadic ones in charity games only. In September 1883, he was elected Rangers president but after only a month felt that he had to resign due to a strange occurrence. In that Victorian era, two umpires, one nominated by each team playing, helped the referee to officiate. In the event of a disputed decision, it was the referee who was the ultimate arbiter. Before a game against Dumbarton, a delegation of Rangers players opposed Vallance's nomination as umpire because they thought that 'Honest Tom' would be too honest, too fair and unbiased, to the detriment of Rangers' chances of winning the match. As a man of honour, Vallance resigned.

By November he was president again, those responsible for his insult having apologised to him. He served the club well until May 1889 when he stepped down as president, this time in more normal circumstances. He should be remembered in any gallery of Rangers greats. Vallance played 122 games for Rangers.

## John McPherson (1891–1902)

Born in Kilmarnock, this prolific goalscorer eventually became a Rangers director. In his 12 seasons as a player, he turned out in every position for the club, even appearing in goal on one occasion. His most familiar shirt, though, was the number-10 shirt. Apart from helping the club to four League titles, he also appeared in three Scottish Cup-winning sides, scoring in two of the Finals. He played 13 times for Scotland, including four appearances against 'the auld enemy', England. On the 50th anniversary of the club's foundation, many Rangers supporters considered him the finest Rangers player to that date. One Victorian hack, John H. Walker, had even called him 'the most natural goalscorer of the 19th century.'

Not only was he a deadly striker, but he was also a great dribbler with the ball who could feint, swerve and elude defenders before unleashing a powerful shot. Despite the passage of over 100 years, McPherson is still in the top five of Rangers' scorers against Celtic. In the inaugural League season of 1890–91, in which he was an ever-present, in the crunch match with soon-to-be joint champions Dumbarton, he scored a vital goal. It was his first game since his wedding and, interestingly, he had thus become the only married Ranger in that side. To show their admiration for McPherson, the club members had a collection and gave him £120 on the occasion of his marriage. That would have been enough to buy a house at that time.

McPherson played 219 games for Rangers and scored 121 goals. He won four League Championships and three Scottish Cups.

## Nicol Smith (1893–1905)

Although he had played a couple of games in the previous season, it was in 1893–94 that the legendary Nicol Smith formed an unforgettable full-back partnership with Jock Drummond, who had established himself in the side at left-back the season before Smith. These two formidable defenders would have fitted perfectly into the 'Iron Curtain' Gers side of the 1950s or rivalled the partnership of Shearer and Caldow from the early 1960s.

At right-back, Smith was what the more polite spectators of the day would have called 'robust' or 'uncompromising'. He was the sort of guy who would have tackled a tank to help his teammates. Apparently, he was very good at utilising the shoulder charge, then an accepted and frequently used method of thwarting opponents. He was also speedy for such a powerful man and was good in the air. His brawn was also complemented by a sense of anticipation and an awareness of danger that saved the day many a time, without him having to resort to brute strength.

In all, Smith gained 12 caps for Scotland and appeared against England on four occasions, dominating the English forwards who thought that they would be too talented for the Scottish defenders. Smith's glorious career ended tragically halfway through the 1904–05 season when he died from a fatal illness on 6 January. He and his wife caught enteric fever and died, leaving behind four children. He had played his last League match less than two months previously.

Nicol Smith played 205 games and scored five goals for Rangers. He won five League Championships and three Scottish Cups.

## Alec Smith (1894–1915)

Left-winger Alec Smith was an Ayrshire man, but this did not stop him from turning down the chance to join Kilmarnock who wanted him before Sunderland came in with an offer. Apparently, the English club would not agree to pay him the £3 a week that he wanted, so instead of joining either club he played a trial with Rangers in a friendly against the, then, English giants Notts County, holders of the

FA Cup, and starred in a 3–1 win at Ibrox. A mere 18-year-old, he was signed and went on to play for 21 seasons for the club. Smith was perhaps the first of the great Rangers left-wingers and deserves to be considered as an equal of later ones such as Alan Morton, Davie Wilson, Willie Johnston, Davie Cooper and Brian Laudrup.

Like all the best wingers, the unselfish Smith had an abundance of skill with brilliant ball control, great pace and the ability to deliver the type of crosses that centre-forwards dream of. He played 20 times for Scotland and won every trophy possible while at Ibrox. A few years after he retired, although his successor on the left wing, Alan Morton, was arguably an even better winger, Rangers fans never forgot the telling contribution made by Alec Smith throughout his Rangers career.

Smith played 239 games and scored 109 goals. He won eight League Championships and two Scottish Cups.

## Jimmy Gordon (1907–20)

Gordon enjoyed a long career at Ibrox despite the fact that in his early days many did not think he had the physical strength to survive the rigours of playing for Rangers. His 334 matches and five League titles proved them wrong. He was a right-half but had a versatility about him that led to him playing at left-back, both wings and even at centre-forward during his time with Rangers. Circumstances conspired to deprive him of that elusive Scottish Cup-winners' medal – those circumstances being the Hampden Riot. In that 1909 Final replay Gordon actually scored the Rangers goal in the 1–1 draw, but due to confusion about whether there would be extra-time or another replay, both Gers and Celtic fans united for once and in their fury at there being no extra-time started a riot. The SFA withheld the trophy for that year, and that was the nearest Gordon got to a winners' medal. Gordon never gained a Scotland cap, but he did play 14 times for the Scottish League side in an era when League Internationals were considered quite important. When he left Ibrox, he went to play for Dunfermline.

Jimmy Gordon played 334 games for Gers and scored 65 goals. He won five League Championships.

## Tommy Cairns (1913–27)

Signed in December 1913, inside-forward Cairns played right into the 1920s for the club. He made his debut against Hamilton and, in all, he played 493 matches and scored 160 goals, and he even captained the side for a while. He gained six Scotland caps. The single failure in a wonderful Ibrox career was that he never got his hands on that treasured Scottish Cup-winners' medal, having retired the year before Rangers broke their Hampden 'hoodoo' by beating Celtic in the Cup Final of 1928. Before that, he played in the losing Cup Finals of 1921 and 1922.

It is easy to see why Cairns lasted so long at Rangers, playing under two managers. He came to exemplify the 'Rangers' Spirit' with his never-say-die attitude and tremendous work ethic. He was the type of player that every top-class team must have if it is to succeed. He was brave, energetic and wily, coupled with a fierce determination. His chunky frame and apparently dour play concealed an intelligent footballing brain that never tired of finding ways of unlocking the most formidable of defences. In his early years at the club, he partnered 'Doc' Paterson on the left wing. Incidentally, the winger really was a doctor, hence the nickname. It was in the 1920s, however, that a legendary partnership was formed with a player who became one of the all-time greats – Alan Morton. Cairns was the brawn, the energy beside the footballing brain of Morton, the genius.

Cairns left Ibrox in 1927 and moved on to Bradford City, where he spent five years. When he retired he was almost 42 years old, an incredible achievement in those days when players were normally thought to be 'over-the-hill' at 30. Most fans would agree that Tommy Cairns was a prime example of a 'true' Ranger who always put the club before personal glory. What a pity he did not win that Scottish Cup medal he so richly deserved. A football pundit of the time, George Neilson, thought that 'it was a tragedy that Cairns never did win that elusive medal.'

Tommy Cairns played 493 games and scored 160 goals. He won six League Championships.

## Andy Cunningham (1914–29)

A couple of years after Cairns had signed for Rangers, he was joined by Andy Cunningham who, for a time in the 1970s, would be revered as the 'oldest living Ranger'. The Ayrshireman was already an established Scottish international when he was brought from Kilmarnock in the spring of 1915, and he would eventually score 163 League goals, enough for him to be number seven in the top 10 of Rangers' League scorers. He played a total of 447 games for Rangers and scored

201 goals in all matches. He also played 12 times for Scotland, and when he left Ibrox he moved to Newcastle United.

Although tall and powerful, Cunningham was also an elegant, graceful forward, who always seemed calm and collected in the hustle and bustle of the penalty area. Not only did he have a fierce shot, but he was also good with his head. He could play as a centre-forward or, like Tommy Cairns, he could perform as an inside-forward who could score goals; although he also had a more skilful approach than Cairns, making him the ideal foil for him in the side. By 1920 Cunningham was an integral part of a magnificent forward line that was admired by fans all over the country: Archibald, Muirhead, Cunningham, Cairns and Paterson. He also survived to become part of an even more renowned forward line that helped win the Scottish Cup for Rangers in 1928: Archibald, Cunningham, Fleming, McPhail and Morton.

Few deserved their Cup medal more, for Cunningham had been in two losing Finals prior to this and in the 1922 Scottish Cup Final against Morton had suffered a broken jaw and been taken off after only 25 minutes' play. It was fitting that such a fine player should avoid the fate of Tommy Cairns and complete his set of domestic medals with Rangers.

Cunningham played 447 games and scored 201 goals. He won seven League Championships and one Scottish Cup.

## Bert Manderson (1915–27)

The big Ulsterman made his debut for Rangers in 1915 against Aberdeen and went on to play for the club for the next 12 years. He was one of the great Gers full-backs, and perhaps his nickname 'Daddy Long Legs' suggests a particular advantage he had when tackling forwards from his right-back berth. For many years he had a great understanding with his left-back, and fellow Ulsterman, Billy McCandless. Such a defensive pairing can be considered right up there with the likes of Shearer and Caldow in the early 1960s.

Manderson was a larger-than-life character, an extrovert who always seemed to play the game for the love of it. His energy and confidence seemed boundless. It would be difficult to imagine him going into a tackle with any malice. It was strange that he only won five caps for Ireland considering the top-class experience he would have provided. Funnily enough, the last of his caps came playing against Scotland – at Ibrox. Most of his Ibrox days were spent as a stalwart in an all-conquering Rangers side, and in his time at the club he won the League Championship seven times but, like so many brilliant teammates of that era, missed out on a Scottish Cup medal. Ironically, in 1927 he left Gers for Bradford City along with his friend Tommy Cairns, so their feelings can be imagined when Rangers won the Scottish Cup the year after their departure.

Manderson played 370 games and scored six goals. He won seven League Championships.

## Tommy Muirhead (1917–30)

In May 1917 Rangers paid Hibs £20 for the services of Muirhead, and it was certainly money well spent as the player went on to perform brilliantly for the club for the next 13 years, eventually captaining the team. He could play as an inside-forward or a wing-half, mainly on the right although for Scotland he had played at left-half as well, earning eight caps. From Cowdenbeath, he was not the first Fifer, or the last, to play for the club. He was a tremendously creative player, in the style of the typical Scottish wing-halves of that time. He was a natural footballer who seemed to have all the attributes to make him a success in the professional game. As well as being a great passer of the ball, he could show a subtlety and flair that would often be enough to win the match for his side. Although primarily an inventive, attacking player, he was also an incisive tackler, and with his will-to-win and Rangers spirit he was the sort of reliable player that every team needs to succeed. When he was at his peak as a player he came to exemplify on the field what it meant to be a Rangers player in the Struth era.

As with so many famous Rangers of that era, however, despite an incredibly successful career, Muirhead missed out on playing in a winning Gers side in a Scottish Cup Final before he retired. He actually played in two losing Finals, in 1922 and 1929, but when Rangers eventually broke their 25-year 'hoodoo' in 1928 he was not in the team. Despite this, the club made sure he received a winners' medal. It was the least they could do for all his sterling service throughout his time at Ibrox.

Muirhead played 353 games and scored 49 goals. He won eight League Championships.

# Sandy Archibald (1917–34)

Archibald was another Fifer who joined Rangers around the same time as Muirhead, and he gave the club even longer loyal service, spending 17 years at Ibrox. He joined Rangers from Raith Rovers, as would the great Jim Baxter over 40 years later. He was arguably the longest-serving right-winger ever to have played for the club.

Wingers in those days had to be brave players, and Archibald was certainly that. He was barrel-chested and a vigorous player who could handle himself, but he was also a skilful, free-running, goalscoring winger and worth his weight in gold. He was the ultimate professional who still holds the all-time record for League appearances for the club with a total of 514 – a figure unlikely to be bettered. It is amazing that he only won eight caps for Scotland.

Archibald's attacking skills could light up many a match, and at his peak he could be relied upon to score an average of 12 goals per season – a good total for an out-and-out winger. It was fitting that towards the end of a trophy-laden career he did manage to win the one medal that had eluded him – a Scottish Cup-winners' medal – from the 1928 Old Firm Final. The icing on his cake was the fact that he scored two goals in the game that smashed the Cup hoodoo forever. Nobody deserved it more than Archibald. Football scribe Richard M. Young remembered being at Hampden that day and 'almost being in tears when Archibald scored his second goal.'

In Rangers' two great League-winning seasons of 1920 and 1921, if the Cups are included, Archibald showed his resilience and consistency by playing in a total of 102 matches and scoring 28 goals.

Archibald played 667 games and scored 162 goals. He won 12 League Championships and three Scottish Cups.

# David Meiklejohn (1919–36)

Skipper for the dramatic 1928 Scottish Cup Final against Celtic, David 'Davie' Meiklejohn was one of the great Rangers captains. His stature and character combined to make him an inspiring leader of men and a formidable presence in the side. A local man, born in Govan, he signed from Maryhill Juniors and gave his all for the club. He was Struth's ideal lieutenant on the field. He played at right-half or, when the occasion demanded it, centre-half, and his ability to read the game as well as tackle made him a difficult obstacle for opponents to circumvent.

Uncompromising, determined, resolute and vigorous are all adjectives that were used to describe Meiklejohn's style, but he was so much more than just a hard defender. He had a footballing brain and a composure that meant he was a natural leader on the park, a player who remained unflustered and who could drive his teammates on to victory. Another, later, Rangers legend, Willie Thornton, said that Meiklejohn was 'the greatest player I've ever seen.'

Meiklejohn's courage, dedication, selflessness and self-belief all came together in that moment when he assumed the responsibility of taking the vital penalty-kick in the 1928 Scottish Cup Final against Celtic to end the 'Hampden Hoodoo'. He was the John Greig of his time, and no higher praise can be given than that. After 17 years, he played his final League game against Hearts at Ibrox in 1936. He was capped 15 times for Scotland and captained his country twice against England. He was the sort of captain that every team needs but few are lucky enough to possess.

Meiklejohn played 635 times for the club, scoring 54 goals. He won 12 League titles as well as five Scottish Cups.

# Chapter Two

# Players Elected Between 1920–54

## History of the Period

Despite the tragic death of manager William Wilton at the end of the 1919–20 season, the next season saw Rangers forge ahead under new manager Bill Struth, who had already made a name for himself as the trainer at the club. He retained the Championship that had been won by Wilton's side, and in the 1920s he built some of Rangers' greatest teams through his unerring ability to spot a player of quality and make use of his talents. The 1920s and 1930s saw Rangers ensconced at the pinnacle of Scottish football. Throughout this era, Struth introduced players to Ibrox who would go on to become legends, but by the end of it, when those players were hanging up their boots, he had made sure that future legends such as Waddell, Thornton, Shaw and Woodburn were already at the club to take their place.

Of the 27 titles up for grabs during this period, Rangers won 18. Indeed, on two occasions a single Championship win by another club ruined what would have been the first nine-in-a-row run. In the worst season in Rangers' history, in which the side finished sixth, Celtic won the title when a win for Gers would have seen nine consecutive Championships won by 1930–31. Equally, if the greatest-ever Motherwell side had not won the title in 1931–32, Rangers would have done nine-in-a-row by 1934–35. Ironically, Rangers came second that season, having accrued more points and scored more goals than the previous two seasons in which the title had been won. In seven seasons the side topped the century mark and twice managed to score an incredible 118 goals in 38 games. As well as this, on two occasions only one defeat was suffered in the entire League campaign. Significantly, each decade ended the way it had started – with a Rangers Championship victory.

Also, in this period, as you might expect, the success rate rose in the Cup competitions, especially the Scottish Cup. When Rangers beat Celtic in the Scottish Cup Final of 1928, it broke an incredible 25-year drought during which many had begun to believe that the club was 'jinxed' in the competition – even under the management of Bill Struth. Jinx or not, from then on the Scottish Cup appeared regularly on the Ibrox honours list. Indeed, after that win, Rangers won the Cup five times in the next 11 seasons.

It was at this time that Rangers won the Scottish Cup for three consecutive years – a feat still very difficult to achieve. In 1934 St Mirren was vanquished, a year later Hamilton and, in 1936, old foes Third Lanark. In the initial days of this competition, before professionalism, only Vale of Leven and Queen's Park (twice) had managed to do this, when the two clubs had been the top dogs in Scottish football. Rangers superseded both by achieving it three times, the last being in the early 1960s. It is an accomplishment that Celtic has never managed, and the only other club to do it was Alex Ferguson's Aberdeen side of the early 1980s. During the inter-war period, the club also won the Glasgow Cup 11 times and the Glasgow Charity Cup 10 times.

As might be expected, some Rangers records were created during this period. The 1927–28 team was the first Gers side to win the double. The team of 1929–30 did the 'Clean Sweep' of League and Scottish Cup, with the Glasgow Cup and Glasgow Charity Cup added for good measure. That season was perhaps the high water mark for the club. In September 1933 Rangers in effect became the unofficial British champions when they beat Arsenal home and away. The 'Bank of England' side, Arsenal, were the aristocrats of the English League – the mirror image of Rangers in Scotland. This tremendous Gunners side, managed by the legendary Herbert Chapman, were in the middle of a three-in-a-row run of English Championships and obviously were a formidable team. Nevertheless, Rangers beat them 2–0 at Ibrox and then 3–1 at Highbury a week later. It was one of those results that had all Scots, especially those who lived in England, purring with pride and holding their heads up high. During the 1930s, Rangers formed a great relationship with Arsenal and in the six games played won three, drew two and lost only one.

When Britain went to war with Germany in September 1939, Rangers topped the League by one point after five matches had been played. Due to government edict, the remainder of the League programme was scrapped and the Scottish Cup suspended for the duration of the war. Eventually, in place of the League, the Scottish Regional League – Western Division was instigated. This consisted of most of the biggest clubs in the country apart from Hearts, Hibs, Aberdeen and Dundee, due to geography. Rangers won this particular competition in the 1939–40 season before another version of the League was devised the following season.

Due to complaints from Hearts and Hibs about their reduction in revenue caused by the lack of games against the Old Firm in particular, they were admitted into the new League which was split north to south. Thus, only Aberdeen and Dundee were missing from the clubs who had competed for the League title prior to the war starting.

In each of the six seasons of this Scottish Southern League, Rangers won the title. Although these are not considered 'proper' League Championships, it has to be said that they were the competitive equivalent of the official pre-war League.

Unfortunately, the World War Two years are not counted in the official records of Scottish football. Some Rangers players saw out the last games of their great careers during this period, while others were just starting out on a memorable one. It should still be remembered, however, that whichever League competition was in operation for that period, Rangers won it.

When official League football started after the war in 1946–47, Rangers began where they had left off prior to the conflict – by winning the Championship.

In the eight post-war seasons under Struth, Rangers won the Championship four times, in an age that had seemed to usher in fiercer competition than at any time in the history of the Scottish League. Proof of this can be seen in the fact that, in that era, Hibs won three Championships and Celtic won one, while a couple of years later Hearts and Aberdeen were also champions. During this spell, Rangers also won the Scottish Cup four times, the newly founded League Cup twice, as well as six Glasgow Cups and six Glasgow Charity Cups.

Rangers' famed 'Iron Curtain' defence was given the credit for many an Ibrox triumph, but the side also contained attacking brilliance in the form of Waddell, Thornton, Gillick and Duncanson. The nickname was an allusion to the term used by Winston Churchill to describe the Soviet Bloc at that time. The expression seemed so appropriate for that Gers' defence as it was similar in that its individual parts held together as a unit, making that unit incredibly difficult to penetrate. The formidable defence, renowned for its meanness, consisted of: Brown; Young, Shaw; McColl, Woodburn, Cox. With injuries perhaps less frequent at that time, this was the defence that played in most matches over a period of seasons. All of those defenders looked as if they had come from the same mould – strong, physical, fit, determined and committed. Every one of them was captain material and every one of them, at some point, captained Rangers. Some even captained Scotland. Two – Brown and McColl – would go on to become Scotland managers.

This period saw Rangers create another couple of 'firsts' for the club. In the 1946–47 season Rangers became the first team to win the newly instigated League Cup by beating Aberdeen 4–0 at Hampden. Two seasons later, Rangers became the first to win what became known as 'The Treble' by succeeding in all three National competitions. Another landmark of this period came in season 1949–50 when a Scottish Cup triumph against East Fife meant Rangers' third consecutive Scottish Cup was secured, a feat seldom achieved. It was the second time the club had managed this, equalling the achievement of Queen's Park who had managed it in the earliest days of the competition. The mid-1950s saw a bit of a hiatus as old age and illness crept up on Bill Struth, causing his Rangers sides to be less than consistent. A 'lowly' fourth-place finish in season 1953–54, the worst Rangers placing since the disastrous season of 1925–26, meant it was the right time for the 81-year-old Struth to resign.

## MANAGER : WILLIAM STRUTH (1920–1954)

In May 1914 one of the most significant events in Rangers' history occurred; although few, then, realised this. The club's trainer of 17 years, Jimmy Wilson, died. A modest, quiet-spoken man, he had been a devoted and diligent servant to Rangers and was much mourned. Nevertheless, the life of any club goes on, and Wilson's replacement would eventually turn out to be the greatest manager in the club's history – William Struth. Struth had been a professional runner before becoming involved with football as the trainer of Clyde. He was a stern disciplinarian and was considered a tyrant, but he was nevertheless respected by the players. His drive and ambition were vital in helping manager William Wilton battle against the dominance of Celtic during the World War One era, and eventually they succeeded.

William Struth portrait.

The bust of Bill Struth, who managed the club from 1920–54, on the landing of the marble stairway.

Born in Kinross-shire in 1875, he spent much of his early years living near Hearts' ground, perhaps resulting in him having a soft spot for the local side. Strangely enough, his background was one of athletics rather than football. In his younger days, he had been a professional runner and always remembered those times as a period in his life when if you did not win, you did not eat. If that does not inculcate a winning mentality into someone, then what could? The rigours of touring the country, having to race for money, certainly helped build his character and shape his outlook on life.

When he joined the club as trainer, Struth had already established a fine reputation while trainer of Clyde, having made them one of the fittest teams in the country. By the time he became Rangers manager he already had the respect and admiration of his players thanks to his ceaseless drive, energy and expertise in tailoring his fitness regimes to individual players in order to get the best out of them. He had studied anatomy and physiotherapy, which helped him understand players' injuries and conditioning so that he could improve their performances by ensuring they were at their peak for each match. Struth was the perfect age, with experience and gravitas in abundance, when he had to take the reins from William Wilton after his tragic and sudden death.

It was Bill Struth, perhaps more than any other single person, who defined Rangers' ethos or spirit. He was driven to ensuring that Rangers would become and stay the country's number-one club and a sporting institution that all those connected with the club would be proud of. And how he succeeded! No manager, probably in any country, at any time, has dominated his country's Championship for as long as Bill Struth did. Apart from the winning of trophies and the pursuit of excellence in his choice of players, Struth set the tone for Rangers and its players.

Struth believed that he was in a privileged position at Ibrox, and his dedication to Rangers could never be questioned, so he expected no less from his staff. Players were trained to be physically fit specimens with the mental strength to compete to their utmost and win prizes. Coming second best was not in Struth's or Rangers' philosophy. One thing was always assured – no Rangers side of Struth's would ever be found wanting in terms of fitness or character, and a later manager, Jock Wallace, would ensure that his sides showed the same virtues.

Struth was not a tactician in football terms. His strengths lay in being able to identify a player whose qualities he could integrate into the side, as well as inspiring the players with encouraging words before the match. Struth instilled a will to win into his players, an absolute belief in their own ability. He believed in having a settled team because consistency of selection led to consistency of performance, which led to ultimate success. He left the on-field tactics and changes to his senior players who knew how to play the game better than he did and whose judgement he trusted because they were 'his boys'. Loyalty at Ibrox was a two-way street. The players trusted 'The Boss' and gave him their loyalty and had this from him in return.

Struth's mission was to give his players the best of everything, from travel arrangements to hotels and food. In return, this man of iron expected them to be fastidious in their dress sense and disciplined in their behaviour, both on and off the field. Indeed, Struth had a wardrobe in his Ibrox office that contained various suits, allowing him to change when the occasion demanded it. Still, if a Rangers player was to receive first-class everything, the least the club could expect in return was impeccable behaviour that would enhance the image of the club. The good name of Rangers was always his primary concern. On his desk, he had a sign that simply said: 'The club is greater than the man.' Nobody doubted that Struth believed this axiom and that he tried to imbue his players with its spirit.

Struth's loyalty and concern for his players is perhaps best encapsulated by an incident that happened during the Scottish Cup Final of 1922 when Rangers lost 1–0 to Morton. During the first half, ace striker Andy Cunningham broke his jaw. So what did the so-called ruthless Struth do? He went with his player to the nearby Victoria Infirmary and stayed with him, missing the rest of the Cup Final. Such loyalty could only be reciprocated by the players over the next 30 years.

Before he resigned as manager due to ill health, he made sure that the club would appoint the successor of his choice, his protégé and former player Scot Symon. As with everything else, Struth was putting the club first in his endeavour to see it continue as the premier club in the country.

Although he had that fierce determination to succeed, Bill Struth knew that it was impossible to win every game, every Championship and every Cup. His philosophy, which many would do well to remember nowadays, was that out of adversity a stronger person or team should emerge. He cautioned that, in the bad times, a sense of 'sanity and tolerance' must be preserved in the confident knowledge that Rangers would come back to their rightful place. Under Struth, for most of his wonderful career, that place was top of the pile, keeping ahead of the others. As this former runner once said, 'Let the others come after us. We welcome the chase'. He died in 1956, aged 81.

During the Struth years, Rangers won 18 League Championships, 10 Scottish Cups, two League Cups, 18 Glasgow Cups and 20 Glasgow Charity Cups.

# *Players Elected*

## Alan Morton (1920–33)

In the Greatest Rangers Team, which was selected a few years ago by the current fans, illogically, two left-wingers were picked for that imaginary side – Davie Cooper and Brian Laudrup. Obviously, due to the very nature of this exercise for electing Rangers' Hall of Fame, the stars from older generations were bound to be at a disadvantage to their more modern counterparts. Great players though they were, most observers with a knowledge of football history would admit that Laudrup and Cooper should not have been picked at the expense of Alan Morton, the greatest of them all.

In terms of money, Morton was the Beckham of his day when Bill Struth, in his first season as manager, finally signed him in 1920 from amateurs Queen's Park. He had been at Hampden since 1913 and worked as a mining engineer, a capacity in which he continued to work throughout his career. His signing-on fee was £3,000 – a massive amount in those days when, as mentioned previously, a car only cost £100 and a house £300. Morton's weekly wage was £60 – the same as some Gers players were earning over 40 years later!

From start to finish, Morton made a huge impact on Rangers and quickly became the club's hero. So wonderful a career did he have that when he retired in 1933 Rangers promptly made him a director of the club. It was a just reward for a magician who played 495 matches and scored 115 goals for Rangers working with Bill Struth at his peak throughout those years. Morton won nine League Championship medals, three Scottish Cups and was even revered by Scotland fans for having played against England on an astonishing 11 occasions, only missing one clash with England (which Scotland lost at Old Trafford) due to injury. He was a famed member of the immortal 'Wembley Wizards' Scotland side of 1928 that

The portrait of legendary winger, and later club director, Alan Morton, at the top of the marble staircase inside Ibrox.

humiliated the English on their own patch, and his total of 31 Scotland caps must be put into perspective for modern readers. In Morton's time, generally, only three international games were played each season, so his final tally was phenomenal.

This brilliant winger had everything: skill, poise, quick reflexes, fast feet, tremendous timing and courage. Apart from this natural ability, as a boy he had spent hours practising with a ball, trying to master it so that it would do his will. And how that paid off! He could get past defenders as if they were not there before delivering a telling cross or deadly cut-back. He tormented English defenders in the same way that, years later, Stanley Matthews would Scotland ones. It was English sportswriter, Ivan Sharpe, who gave him one of his nicknames that put fear into English players and fans alike – 'The Wee Blue Devil'.

Around Ibrox, however, his nickname was 'The Wee Society Man', no doubt stemming from his immaculate appearance as he walked into Ibrox each day for training dressed in a suit while wearing gloves and a bowler hat. He personified Rangers' image off the field, and on it he moved with a grace and skill that generated excitement among the fans and was emulated by many legendary Rangers wingers in the future, but never surpassed. How fitting that the huge oil painting of Alan Morton (in his Scotland jersey) dominates the famed marble staircase of Ibrox, reminding the various generations of this player's genius. He served the club loyally as a director until shortly before his death in 1971.

Morton played 495 games and scored 115 goals. He won nine League Championships and three Scottish Cups.

## Dougie Gray (1925–47)

Dougie Gray had the misfortune to join Rangers from Junior side Aberdeen Mugiemoss in June 1925, just before the most disastrous season in the club's history when the side finished sixth in the League Championship; however, that one season was an aberration in the defender's career as well as in the history of Rangers. In his following 22 seasons with the club Gray would go on to win 11 League Championships and six Scottish Cups. He also played for Scotland on 10 occasions.

Gray was a fine player, if not a legendary one, but his fame continues due to his longevity. He is still the club record-holder for League and Cup appearances, with a massive total of 667. If all matches are counted, he played in an awesome 940 games. His was a glittering career that few have surpassed.

For a defender in those days, Gray was not a huge presence. He was a right-back of moderate stature whose mobility, quick thinking and vision allowed him to make interceptions rather than fierce tackles in order to prevent the opposition threatening his goal. At the time, it was said of him that he had cleared more shots off his goalline than any defender known to the fans until then. His defending was always composed and resolute. Like all the Gers players of his era, he had the mental strength to do his utmost for the team and battle on, no matter what.

It was a pity that the last few years of his career spanned World War Two when League titles and goals scored were traditionally excluded from the official records. When he retired at the end of the 1946–47 season, who could have thought that, almost 60 years later, he would still be the Ranger who had played most games for the club? He played 667 games, winning 11 League Championships and six Scottish Cups.

## Bob McPhail (1927–40)

During his first season at Ibrox, prolific goalscorer Bob McPhail was able to tease his new teammates that he was the only player in the dressing room with a Scottish Cup-winners' medal. He had won this in 1924 when he was an Airdrie star, but by the end of that first season, by scoring one of the goals in the 1928 Cup Final, McPhail had helped bring to an end that reason for having fun at his mates' expense.

When Rangers captured the big striker from Airdrie it was quite a coup because half a dozen top English clubs were also chasing his signature. A Scottish international schoolboy player, McPhail was a big, powerful lad who had won his Scottish Cup medal with Airdrie when he was only 18. He would go on to win six more with Rangers as well as help the club to nine League Championships. If Jimmy Smith's 74 wartime goals are excluded, McPhail was Rangers' top League goalscorer of all time with 230 – until the arrival on a certain Ally McCoist at Ibrox, that is, who overtook that total in the 1990s. His record had lasted for over half a century, and he was still alive to see it broken.

When McPhail joined Rangers, he had the unenviable task of taking over the number-10 shirt from the inimitable Tommy Cairns, who had formed a devastating left-wing partnership with Alan Morton. Soon, though, McPhail's scoring exploits were creating a new hero for the Ibrox legions. Of course, it was not only his natural ability, dedication and tremendous work-rate that led to so many goals, he was also playing in a brilliant side surrounded by a lot great players. With two tremendous wingers in Archibald and Morton supplying the ammunition, and another couple of goalscorers in Fleming and Cunningham who had to be watched by defenders, is it any wonder McPhail managed to score so freely?

As with all truly great strikers, McPhail had the requisite qualities of courage and determination. Before the 1934 Scottish Cup Final against St Mirren, McPhail had been suffering from a groin injury. So vital a player was he that Bill Struth decided that he was fit enough to play provided he was strapped up with a huge bandage. McPhail was willing to give it a try but mentioned to his boss that he would not be able to lift his leg up very high, to which Struth replied, 'Maybe so, but St Mirren won't know that!'. McPhail played and scored one of the goals in a 5–0 demolition of the Paisley Buddies.

Striker Bob McPhail's collection of medals won during the 1920s and 1930s.

Apart from a few seasons when injury limited his appearances, bustling Bob guaranteed Rangers 20–30 goals a season, so it is no wonder that it took the extraordinary striking power of another goalscoring Rangers legend, Ally McCoist, to eventually surpass McPhail's totals.

McPhail played 466 games, scoring 281 goals. He won nine League Championships and six Scottish Cups with Gers, as well as one with Airdrie.

## Jimmy Smith (1928–46)

Jimmy Smith is one of the least known of the true Rangers greats but is nevertheless a player who deserves far greater respect than he was ever accorded until his death in 2003. Smith's tragedy was that, as in the case of Dougie Gray, the final years of his career at Ibrox took place during World War Two when matches played and goals scored were not considered official. Smith scored a total of 73 League goals alone during the war, making his career League total 300 – 63 and 67 ahead of McCoist and McPhail respectively. Even omitting his wartime strikes, Smith is still the third most prolific League goalscorer in the club's history. Taking all his games into account, however, nobody has scored more goals for Rangers than this man.

Built like a heavyweight boxer, standing over 6ft tall and weighing around 14st, Smith was a fearsome forward to have to defend against. As you might expect, this tank of a man was adept at using his power to the side's advantage. He was considered one of the greatest exponents of the shoulder charge, and the less-protected 'keepers of his era knew that better than anyone. Smith might have been a battering ram, but he also had a deft touch and could link up well with his fellow forwards.

Although he joined Rangers in 1928, having only played a dozen games for East Stirlingshire but scoring 16 goals, it was not until March 1929 until he made his first-team debut at Hamilton. At that time the great Jimmy Fleming was holding down the number-nine shirt, so it was not until the 1930–31 season that Smith took possession of it. In fact, this had probably been helped by the successful close-season tour of North America that Rangers had made prior to that season. During that tour, Smith had scored 18 goals in 14 matches and no doubt had convinced Bill Struth that he was ready for first-team duty. He never looked back. He ended up winning six League Championships and three Scottish Cups.

Apart from a couple of seasons when the prolific scorer Sam English was creating a record of 44 League goals, Smith was a fixture in the Gers side. He managed 41 League goals in the 1933–34 season, 36 goals the next season and 31 in each of the following two seasons. What a forward to have playing beside Bob McPhail!

## Sam English (1931–33)

When Sam English was inducted into Rangers' Hall of Fame in 2009 no doubt many discerning Gers fans with a knowledge of the club's history gave a smile of satisfaction. They remembered English as perhaps the most tragic figure in Rangers' history. Sam English was unique for a few reasons: his fame was inextricably linked with that of a Celtic star, he holds a goalscoring record that stands to this day and he is the Hall of Fame member with the fewest appearances for the club.

Sam, from Ulster, had English as a surname but was best known in Scotland, even though his spell at Ibrox was brief. He was born in 1908 in Coleraine and as a young man had arrived in Glasgow to work in the shipyards. It was while playing for the Junior club Yoker, near the shipyard, that he drew the attention of a Rangers scout who was impressed by his prolific goalscoring exploits. At the age of 23, in July 1931, he signed for Rangers.

His first season at Ibrox led to English establishing a goalscoring record that has never been beaten – not even by Rangers' record goalscorer Ally McCoist. In that season, English scored an incredible 44 goals in 35 League appearances. Add the nine he scored in the Scottish Cup, including one in the Final replay, when Gers beat Kilmarnock 3–0, and the total of 53 is quite remarkable. Ironically, English's massive tally could not help Rangers to the League Championship that season as Motherwell beat them to the title. Normal service was resumed the following season, however, when the League positions were reversed. What a pity that Well's title win was all that prevented Rangers from becoming the first side to win nine-in-a-row.

English made an immediate impact on his new club by scoring seven goals in his first two League matches. In his debut against Dundee he scored with two headers in a 4–1 win but eclipsed that with five goals in his next game against Morton who were beaten 7–3. The next striker to create such an initial impact was arguably Colin Stein 37 years later, when he started his Ibrox career with two hat-ticks and a double in his third game.

At only 5ft 8in tall, English was not a big, strong, bustling type of centre-forward, but he was fast and had a natural instinct for goalscoring. There is no doubt he was aided in his scoring prowess by playing in a brilliant Rangers team that dominated the 1930s as it had the 1920s. His strike partner was the legendary Bob McPhail who was at his peak when English was introduced to the side. He was also fortunate to have attacking colleagues of the stature of veteran Sandy Archibald and Jimmy Fleming. His scoring ability was recognised by gaining his two Northern Ireland caps at that time.

In English's second season, while McPhail's goal tally was 29 in 31 matches, English only managed 10 in 25 League appearances. This disparity between English's first and second season's goal exploits can be attributed to one circumstance – the death of Celtic goalkeeper, John Thomson. It is with this terrible tragedy that Sam English will be forever linked. While some fans are aware of English's League goals in a season record, more will know of him as the player with whom Thomson collided, resulting in his death at the age of 22.

The incident happened on 5 September 1931, five minutes into the second half of the Old Firm game at Ibrox. At the end of a Rangers attack a cross came over from the right wing for Sam English to run on to. It looked like a certain goal but Celtic 'keeper Thomson was characteristically brave, if not slightly reckless, and came diving out, headlong, at English's feet. The 'keeper saved a goal but his head collided with the knee of English's standing leg as he shot. Thomson lay unconscious, and English could see how serious it was as he checked on the 'keeper and summoned immediately for medical help from the sidelines.

The Celtic icon was stretchered off and was examined by a doctor who had been a spectator in the crowd. Despite the doctor suggesting that Thomson's injury might prove to be fatal, the match was played to a finish. Meanwhile, Thomson was taken to the Victoria Infirmary but never regained consciousness and died that evening from a depressed fracture of the skull.

Celtic lost an international 'keeper that, day and in a way Rangers lost what could have been one of their greatest-ever goalscorers. Thomson's death destroyed Sam English's career. Even after the Fatal Accident Enquiry had found English completely blameless in the incident, the player, ever after, was taunted by opposition supporters. In his first match at Parkhead, Celtic fans could be heard shouting 'murderer' and 'killer'. Even more shamefully, at the enquiry, Celtic manager Willie Maley, when giving evidence, said that he had not seen the collision but 'I hope it was an accident.'

At the end of his second season, English moved on to play for Liverpool, hoping for a fresh start. It was not to be. Crass supporters can be found everywhere, and the abuse continued even in England. Two years later, he moved to Queen of the South before finishing his career at Hartlepool. He could take no more and quit at the age of 28.

When John Thomson was buried, 30,000 mourners attended the ceremony, but in 1967 when Sam English died of motor neurone disease his funeral at Cardross Crematorium, Dunbartonshire, was attended by only a handful of people as his death all but went unnoticed. When he died, Sam English was working as a sheet metal worker in Clydebank. His life had been changed irrevocably by John Thomson's death. How true his comment was that he 'was the second unluckiest footballer in the world.'

Sam English deserves his place in Rangers' Hall of Fame for holding the record for the number of League goals scored in one season. But for Fate, he would surely have added many more.

English played 81 games and scored 72 goals. He won one League Championship and one Scottish Cup.

## Jerry Dawson (1931–45)

Until Andy Goram was voted the greatest Rangers goalkeeper of all time, most older Gers fans would have accorded that honour to Jerry Dawson – 'Prince of Goalkeepers'. Few people seem to know that his real first name was James and that he was tagged 'Jerry' as a nickname, after the England and Burnley 'keeper of the same name who had played some years prior to him.

A Falkirk man, Dawson was signed by Rangers in 1929 from Camelon Juniors and, as understudy to the great Tom Hamilton, it took him until the 1931–32 season to start making regular appearances for the first team. Indeed, his first Old Firm match was, tragically, the one at Ibrox in which Celtic's 'keeper John Thomson was killed in an accidental clash with Sam English. Whereas Celtic lost a legend that day, Rangers found one. Throughout the 1930s and early 1940s Dawson was unquestionably the Rangers' last line of defence.

Dawson was a 'keeper who inspired confidence in his defenders thanks to his genial personality and his qualities as a goalkeeper. He was unflappable, commanded his penalty box and had the type of quick reflexes that only the best 'keepers can display consistently. Alert, mobile and utterly dependable, he was a rock in Rangers' defence that kept the back door closed while the brilliant forward players used their skills to win matches.

Dawson played 14 times for Scotland leading up to World War Two, and by the time he moved from Rangers, after 16 years, he had amassed five League titles and two Scottish Cup medals. When he broke his leg in 1944, considered the worst injury a footballer could suffer in those days, many thought that he would not make a comeback, but he did. He was back in action the following year and fittingly played his final match against the famed Moscow Dynamo side that visited Ibrox in 1945 – opposite another wonderful 'keeper, 'Tiger' Komich. After this match, he signed for his local club Falkirk, and he played there until he retired in 1949.

One of the indisputable Rangers greats, Jerry Dawson died in 1977, still revered by Rangers fans the world over.

Dawson played 211 games and won five League Championships and two Scottish Cups.

## Torry Gillick (1933–35 & 1946–50)

Modern Rangers fans have become used to discussing Gers players with names such as Lorenzo, Gio, Sasha, Jean-Claude and even Nigel, but in the 1930s, when players tended to have names like Billy or Bobby, Torry Gillick stood out because of his unusual first name – Torrance. Always called Torry, he was an extrovert character as befitting his name. As you can see from his dates, he was the only player ever re-signed by Bill Struth. In those days, when you left Rangers it was considered downhill all the way and with no road back. The fact that Gillick played before and after World War Two for Rangers is testimony to the high regard in which he was held.

Although born in Airdrie, it was from Glasgow Junior club Petershill that Gillick signed for Rangers in 1933 as an 18-year-old. Gillick was the classic Scottish inside-forward. He showed wonderful ball control and sense of positioning, coupled with great vision that allowed him to spray superb passes to either wing or through the centre. His service to the other forwards was impeccable and resulted in many a goal. His speciality pass was the one made inside a full-back for the likes of a winger like Waddell to run on to and either score or set up a goal with a cut-back.

This talent was invaluable in itself, but Gillick added to this by having the ability to score goals as well. He was sturdily built and not quick over longer distances, but he did have a speed off the mark that gained him time to damage the opposition by creating or scoring goals. He was always considered a bit of a moaner on the field – rather like Ian Ferguson in the 1990s – but was well-liked by friend and foe alike, on and off the pitch.

In his pre-war, two-year spell at Ibrox, Gillick won the Scottish Cup in 1935 before being transferred to Everton for £8,000. While there, he won the English League title in 1938–39 and became a popular figure at Goodison. During the war, he became a guest player for Rangers. This was a common occurrence during the war, allowing star players to play for other clubs, although the matches played were deemed to be 'unofficial'. Unfortunately for Gillick, his service to Rangers during this period is recorded as unofficial, thus his 207 wartime matches, coupled with his 124 goals, do not 'count' – although they always counted as far as Rangers fans were concerned. Probably his greatest tragedy is that his peak years came during the war.

At the end of World War Two, Bill Struth signed Gillick for a second time. It was no great surprise considering the valuable service the player had given to the club throughout the hostilities. Gillick signed just in time (although this was disputed by the Russians) to face the great Moscow Dynamo side that was touring Britain as a 'goodwill' exercise towards its wartime allies. Gillick will always be remembered for the part he played in that iconic match that ended in an honourable 2–2 draw at Ibrox – a game for which thousands stayed off work or school to see. It had been agreed prior to the game that the new-fangled idea of substitutes should be used. So, at one point, the Russians put on a substitute and the game carried on. It was the ever-alert Gillick who eventually noticed that Rangers were playing against 12 players. The opposition had conveniently forgotten to take a player off! Gillick informed the ref and the matter was remedied.

Gillick went on to have a successful career at Ibrox until 1950, becoming the only Rangers player to win the Scottish Cup before and after World War Two. He gained a winners' medal in the first-ever League Cup Final, scoring one of the goals against Aberdeen. He also scored in his other winning League Cup Final against

Raith Rovers, and he played in Rangers' first side to win the now possible treble in season 1948–49. When he left he was much missed by the Rangers fans, and when he died at the early age of 56 he was much mourned. Ironically, when he died on 12 December 1971 it was on the same day as that other Rangers icon from an earlier era, Alan Morton.

Gillick played 140 games and scored 62 goals (plus wartime of 207 and 124 goals). He won two League Championships, two Scottish Cups and two League Cups.

## Alex Venters (1933–46)

Chunky, broad-chested Venters was one of those players described by hacks as an 'iron man' of the team. He was a brave, hard-working, assertive inside-forward who had a knack for scoring goals – and great ones at that. Yet another great Ranger who was from the Kingdom of Fife, Venters signed in November 1933. He was unfortunate in that the final years of his Rangers career coincided with World War Two. On the other hand, 1933 was a fantastic time to join the club as in season 1933–34 Rangers did the 'Clean Sweep', meaning they won everything that was available to win that season.

An indication of the player's quality was that he was actually a Scotland player while playing for Cowdenbeath in his native Fife. Somehow he was only awarded another two caps in the rest of his career. Despite his undoubted quality, apparently the player had doubts initially about making it at Ibrox once he had joined the long list of household names that made up the Ibrox playing squad at that time. Manager Bill Struth, however, had great faith in the player, and it was not long before he showed his talent and became a success.

Venters won two consecutive Scottish Cup medals in the Finals of 1935 against Hamilton and 1936 against Third Lanark. During the war, he was sent off in curious circumstances. In a Charity Cup match against Celtic at Ibrox in 1940, which Gers won 5–1, in disgust at a decision by the ref Venters booted the ball behind the goal. Unfortunately, it was at the 'Celtic end', the Broomloan end. The ref ordered Venters to go and retrieve the ball. Alex duly tried, but as he went towards the terracing the Celtic fans greeted him with a hail of bottles and missiles. Venters retreated to the pitch, where the ref told him to go back for the ball. Venters refused and was promptly sent off.

An indication of Venters's goalscoring prowess can be confirmed by a couple of facts: despite playing over 60 years ago, he is still ninth in the top 10 Rangers League goalscorers with 155 (including wartime), and in terms of Old Firm matches, he is fifth top with 18 goals. His goals and his skill in creating goals for others were prime assets for Rangers over a span of 13 years. He died in 1959 from a heart attack at the tragically young age of 45 but will be remembered forever in the Hall of Fame.

He played 396 games and scored 188 goals. He won four League Championships and two Scottish Cups.

## Willie Thornton (1936–54)

Willie Thornton was a year older than Willie Waddell when he made his Gers debut, playing for the reserves in 1936; however, perhaps because he was that year older than Waddell, he made his first-team debut before his friend and future attacking partner. On 2 January 1937 he played his debut first-team game against Thistle at Firhill. The teenager, who would score so many goals for Rangers during his career, surprisingly started in this match as an outside-right, helping his side win 1–0.

Born in Winchburgh, West Lothian, Thornton was a precocious teenager and had already played in a trial match for Rangers when a posse of clubs were anxious to sign him, especially Hearts. Luckily, his brother Jimmy was a Rangers fan, and when he heard of Hearts' serious interest in Willie, he phoned Bill Struth to alert him to that fact. The perceptive Struth promptly arranged for him to sign for Rangers before he could be tempted by any other club.

Like Waddell, Thornton was another youngster who quickly discovered what it meant to be a Ranger under Bill Struth. Not only did he become a great scorer for the club, but eventually he was also assistant manager to Waddell and later Rangers' public relations officer. Apart from spells when he managed Dundee and then Thistle, Thornton was a true Ranger for all his life.

Willie Thornton will always be renowned among Rangers fans for his superb aerial ability, and it is true to say that he was a wonderful header of the ball, a player whose timing meant that he met a cross at the optimum moment and ahead of any defender. He also had the technique and ability to hammer the ball towards goal with his head as well as guide it craftily into the net. Arguably, because of this ability his quality on the ground has often been underestimated. He was a mobile forward with great vision and the ability to link up the forward line with his accurate, perceptive passing. A good first touch also helped him control the ball and make valuable time for himself inside the penalty box.

Although every inch a gentleman whom nobody would ever take umbrage with during a game, Thornton was a very courageous man as well as centre-forward. He fought during the war in North Africa and Italy and in 1943 won the Military Medal for his bravery during the Allied invasion of Sicily.

Such qualities saw him play 432 matches for Rangers and score 255 goals. At his peak he was usually good for at least 20 League goals per season. Even now, with 144 goals he is number six in Rangers' top 10 League goalscorers. A paltry total of seven Scotland caps, even allowing for the interruption of the war, leads one to believe that maybe a committee of selectors picking the international side was not that great an idea at any time in our history. To make up for that, however, Thornton did win everything was that was there to be won during his career. He was a member of the team that won the first-ever League Cup and, two seasons later, the first Rangers side to win the now possible treble, scoring 34 goals that season. A modest, unassuming man, his quote that best sums up his temperament and career in goalscoring might be this: 'I never troubled how they went in – so long as they went in for Rangers.'

He won four League Championships, three Scottish Cups and three League Cups.

## Willie Waddell (1936–55)

In March 1936, the 15-year-old Willie Waddell made his debut for Rangers Reserves against Partick Thistle. Doing likewise was the 16-year-old Willie Thornton who, in the future, would often be on the scoring end of a Waddell cross. Few realised then that the young Waddell would leave his mark on the club in such an indelible manner. Waddell not only became an international right-winger for Rangers, but also, eventually, he became the club's manager, general manager and managing director. He was also the spiritual architect of the modern Ibrox Stadium.

One of the great Rangers traditions that has never seemed to get the press coverage it deserves has been the club's ability to produce great wingers who thrill the vast crowds that watch them. Rangers has always had brilliant wingers – of all creeds, nationalities and types. Scots, English, Dutch, Danes, Swedes and South Africans are among those who have sped down the wings. Generally, wingers were categorised into two kinds: the 'tanner ba' sort like Willie Henderson who used trickery, pace and great ability to twist and turn with the ball seemingly stuck to their feet, bamboozling defenders, or ones like Willie Johnston whose sheer pace got them past their opponents. Of course, in-between you had players who combined many of those qualities such as Alan Morton, Alex Scott, Tommy McLean, Brian Laudrup and Mark Walters, to name but a few.

Waddell was the latter type of winger who used power and pace to get into the danger area and send over wonderful crosses for his forwards. His determination, bravery, will to win and fitness also made him one of the greatest wingers to have played for Rangers. He was instilled with the Rangers spirit right from the start, and when he became manager of the club he made sure that the Rangers traditions that he had learned under the tutelage of Bill Struth were continued. Waddell believed, like Struth, that no man was bigger than the club.

He certainly had confidence in his own ability, even at an early age. When he made his first-team debut in 1938 at Ibrox against the mighty Arsenal, not only did he play well but he also scored the only goal of the match. He was 17 years

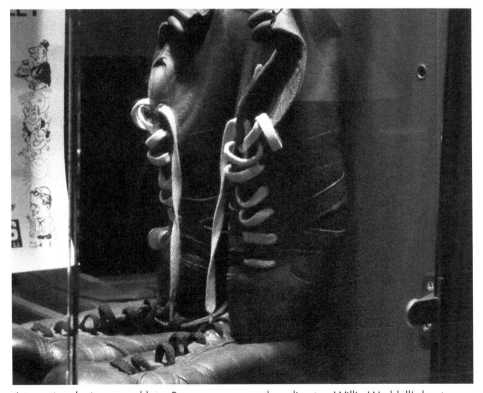

International winger, and later Rangers manager then director, Willie Waddell's boots.

Willie Waddell's shirt.

old. In all, he would go on to play 558 games for Rangers, scoring 143 goals – a good rate for an out-and-out winger. At his peak, Waddell was a winger who could never be left unguarded for a moment. To do so was to risk a counter-attack with him breaking quickly down the wing before sending over a precise cross that would be converted by the likes of Thornton. His determination and courage meant that even a hard-tackling back who tried to intimidate him would fail. Waddell would simply roll up his sleeves and come back for more while 'wiring in' when he had the chance to get his revenge.

Waddell won four League Championships, two Scottish Cups and played 17 times for Scotland, as well as making nine wartime caps.

## Jock Shaw (1938–53)

Jock Shaw might only have been 5ft 7in, weighing in at 11 stones, but, as his nickname suggests, he was a most formidable defender. 'Tiger' Shaw sums him up. This referred not only to his tackling ability but also a steely determination that meant no cause was ever lost while he was still on the pitch. He was one of the great Rangers captains – and there have been many – skippering his side to that first treble among other triumphs. His 16 years at Ibrox saw him retire at the age of 42 with two other top division clubs wanting his signature as a player.

Shaw was another player in the Struth mould. Fit, speedy, gritty and reliable, his durability and hard tackling made him an unwelcome obstacle in the way of any winger. He was the seemingly indestructible left-back in the famed 'Iron Curtain' defence and looked the equal of brilliant players such as Woodburn and Young. It goes without saying that bravery and determination were also qualities that endeared him to his manager and the fans.

Apparently, during one Ne'er Day Old Firm game at Celtic Park, in a clash with Celtic legend Charlie Tully he sustained a bad injury that meant he had to be carried off the field for his leg to be examined. He could barely move the damaged leg, but he pleaded with Bill Struth to be allowed to return to the action and help out his teammates. Struth, always one to take care of his players, refused to allow this and merely told him that the remaining 10 would just work that little bit harder to make up for his loss. Rangers won the match 4–1.

Shaw played 237 games and his haul of medals came to four League Championships, three Scottish Cups and two League Cups. He only played four times for Scotland but captained his country on each occasion.

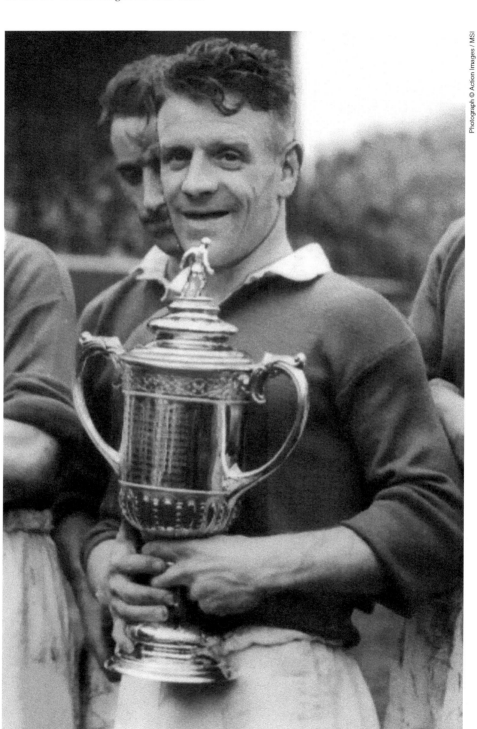

Captain Jock Shaw.

Photograph © Action Images / MSI

# Willie Woodburn (1938–54)

Woodburn's tragedy is that the way his career ended usually gets more attention paid to it than his actual career. A Draconian *sine die* ban from the SFA in 1955 virtually ended his footballing career. On the plus side, he was 35 at that time so he had enjoyed a long and illustrious playing career that was not really tarnished by his ban as the huge majority of fans and pundits recognised how unnecessarily brutal his punishment had been. Nevertheless, it still managed to take the focus away from this player's brilliance.

Rangers signed Woodburn, a Hearts fan, from Musselburgh Athletic in 1937 at the age of 18, and by the 1939–40 season he was a fixture in the side at centre-half. He would go on to become the pivotal figure in the wonderful 'Iron Curtain' defence that served Rangers so well for so many years. Tall, muscular, agile and athletic, 'Big Ben' was supreme in the air but also mobile on the ground, with a great sense of balance that gave him the ability to tackle strongly or use his anticipation and vision to intercept danger. He had a fierce will to win and drive about him that could lead to him taking it out on his colleagues, never mind his opponents, but he was never considered a 'dirty player'. Perhaps rather surprisingly, he was assured in possession of the ball and would pass his way out of defence rather than merely hoofing the ball upfield in the style of most defenders of that era. In truth, he played more like a modern central-defender in the mould of a Frank de Boer but with much more power in the air and on the ground.

A big advantage he had over most fellow defenders and opponents was the fact that hours of practice as a schoolboy had helped him become a two-footed player and be comfortable with the ball at his feet. Most observers at the time considered him a 'stylish' player, especially for a defender, so it is particularly galling that modern fans who never saw him probably only think of him as some kind of 'hard man'.

His final sending off had only been his fifth one – a less-than-startling statistic for modern players. It was always presumed that his severe ban was more for the violence of his last offence than for the number of times he had been up before 'the beaks'. So, what was his heinous offence? In a match at Ibrox against Stirling Albion, with Rangers in control and winning 2–0, he was fouled by Paterson and twisted his leg as he fell to the ground. Woodburn had always been known for his short fuse and, believing the foul to have been deliberate, he got up and gave the offender a 'Glasgow kiss'.

The head-butt was not a form of conduct looked on kindly by the middle-class gents who ran the SFA, so a harsh punishment might have been expected; however, nobody expected the indefinite ban that was issued. Although it was lifted two and a half years later, by that time Woodburn was 38 and out of the game. It had been an ignominious way to have his career ended, leaving such a peerless centre-half devastated.

Woodburn won 24 caps for Scotland, and his medal tally at Ibrox in 325 matches amounted to four League Championships, four Scottish Cups and two League Cups.

## George Young (1941–57)

Born in Grangemouth in 1922, Young would go on to become not only a great Rangers captain but also a great Scotland one. Gers signed him in 1941, from Junior side Kirkintilloch Rob Roy, when he was only 18, realising that his physique and ability would make him the ideal player to build a defence around. At 6ft 2in, weighing 15 stones, he had the presence of a heavyweight boxer. He was regarded as a 'colossus of a man', and when people called him that they were not just referring to his physical stature. As might be expected, he was very powerful in the air and with those long legs he seemed capable of always stretching one out at the right time to make a tackle. He was not just a 'stopper', as he displayed a great ability to use a variety of long-range, accurate passing to start up attacks involving Willie Waddell and Willie Thornton in particular.

Although he was really a centre-half, Young moved to right-back to accommodate the brilliant Willie Woodburn, and big 'Corky' looked entirely comfortable in either berth. Early in his career, through the war years, he was normally played at centre-half, but once normality returned after the conflict he became the regular right-back with Woodburn at centre-half. It mattered not. From either position he commanded the field of play and inspired his teammates. His nickname came about because of his habit of carrying a champagne cork about in his pocket for good luck. How it worked! Apart from his qualities on the field as a player, Young was Bill Struth's alter ego on the pitch, and as a born leader he made sure that the boss's wishes were carried out while also improvising tactics himself.

His worth for the national team was also unsurpassed. Until the arrival of one Alistair McCoist, Young was Rangers' most capped played for Scotland. Proof of

George Young presenting a trophy at Largs in April 1955.

how invaluable he was to Scotland can be seen in the fact that he captained his country eight times against England, played in 53 matches and captaining the side in 48 of those, while being recognised as Scotland's skipper for six consecutive seasons. By the time he had retired in 1957 he had played in the new era of football involving European competition and under the management of a former teammate, Scot Symon, a player he had recognised from early days as a potential manager of the club. Young had played 678 matches for Rangers and been a devoted servant from his teenage days.

George Young won six League Championship medals, four Scottish Cups and two League Cups. His place in Rangers' Hall of Fame was assured.

## Ian McColl (1945–60)

Stylish wing-half Ian McColl, like Bobby Brown, went on to become the Scotland manager after his playing days were over. Another thing McColl had in common with Brown was the fact that he moved to Ibrox from Queen's Park in 1945 to become another lynchpin of the 'Iron Curtain'.

Rangers signed him as an 18-year-old, but he had already been playing for Queen's Park for almost two years, so outstanding a prospect was he. Tall, strong and athletic, he was a defensive right-half who could be relied upon to break up the opposition attacks with his resolute tackling and keen sense of anticipation. He was a hard tackler but he was certainly no 'hard man'. His strength was matched by his brains as there was always a thoughtfulness about his play. He was also very proficient at long-range, accurate passing that could convert defence into attack. Cultured and intelligent were just two of the adjectives used frequently to describe his style of play.

He was intelligent both on and off the field, combining his studies at Glasgow University, taking an engineering degree, with his career as a part-time player. His natural intellect and acquired football nous made it inevitable that he would become a manager after he quit playing and this he duly did, becoming the Scotland manager for four and a half years in the early 1960s when the national side contained some of the country's best-ever players. After that he spent some years as the Sunderland manager before giving up the game altogether.

McColl made 14 appearances for Scotland and 526 as a Ranger, winning six League Championships, five Scottish Cups and two League Cups.

## Sammy Cox (1946–55)

When Sammy Cox was inducted into the Hall of Fame, at the ceremony, you could see how touched he was as he was presented with his honour in front of an adoring audience of former players and fans. Despite having emigrated to Canada almost 50 years previously, he still had his Scots accent, and his first words were 'Once a bluenose, always a bluenose!' The fact that he had come all the way across the Atlantic for the ceremony proved that.

Cox had come a long way. He was an Ayrshire man, born in Darvel in 1924. During World War Two, as a teenager, he had played for Queen's Park, Third Lanark and Dundee. In 1946 he was transferred to Rangers – just in time to become a mainstay of what became one of the greatest Rangers sides of all time, known for its famous 'Iron Curtain' defence. Cox could play at either left-back or left-half and was the equal of those other legends (all of whom are in the Hall of Fame) who made up that unforgettable and largely impregnable defence: Brown; Young, Shaw; McColl, Woodburn, Cox. A sign of Cox's versatility, though, was that he could also play on the right as well as playing in an attacking role. For example, he once played as a left-winger against Clyde and even scored the winning goal. Once, at international level, he played for Scotland against France in Paris at inside-left.

Although only 5ft 8in tall and weighing less than 11st, Cox was a great tackler who may not have been as powerful as teammates like Young, Shaw or Woodburn but he was an intelligent, skilful player whose technique, timing, sense of anticipation and positioning made him a formidable opponent who complemented the others in that celebrated 'Iron Curtain'. It must also be said that the Gers team of that era was not simply a tremendous defence but also had gifted attacking players. For instance, the forward line that won the Scottish Cup in 1948 defeating Morton after a replay, consisted of: Rutherford, Thornton, Williamson, Duncanson, Gillick – not a bad other half of a team!

Cox was also a very resilient and durable character. Proof of this can be seen in the fact that in the 1947–48 season he played in every League game and then the following season he missed only one League match. His first Scottish Cup medal came in that replayed Final of 1948 against Morton, and in the following two Finals against Clyde and East Fife he ran out a winner, making him still one of the few players to have won three consecutive Scottish Cup-winners' medals. He was also a member of the first Rangers (and Scottish) team to win the domestic treble. It was in that season that he won his only League Cup medal, Rangers beating Raith Rovers 2–0 in 1949.

Cox's football brain, tactical sense and ability to tackle in a hard but fair manner ensured that few wingers ever got the better of him – and this was in an era of brilliant wingers. From 1949–54 he was a regular in the international team, eventually playing 24 times for Scotland at a time when there were fewer caps to be won by players. He also captained Scotland against England at Hampden in 1954. Even the best English wingers of all time, Stanley Matthews and Tom Finney, could not overcome the redoubtable Cox – which is perhaps the finest testimony to this true blue's ability.

Cox won three League Championships, three Scottish Cups and one League Cup. He played 310 games for Rangers and scored 20 goals. He also played 24 times for Scotland.

## Bobby Brown (1946–56)

If you are privileged enough to have a chat with an 'old timer' of a Rangers fan who had been following the club since the late 1930s (and there are still a few around), then I bet if you asked him to name his top three Rangers 'keepers, this would be his order: Goram, Dawson, Brown. Yes, Bobby Brown was that good! His election to the Rangers Hall of Fame recently proved that he had not been forgotten by the supporters.

The season following the retirement of the legendary Jerry Dawson in 1945 saw Brown become Gers' number one. He was a P.E. teacher who played part-time for Queen's Park, and after the war, when he was leaving 'The Spiders', he could have signed for Manchester United as Matt Busby was a great admirer of him. He chose to sign for Bill Struth, however, coincidentally on the same day as the club brought in stalwart Sammy Cox, thus adding two vital pieces to what would become known as the 'Iron Curtain' defence.

With his curly, blond hair, the good-looking Brown was a striking-looking athlete, and his style of goalkeeping was unassuming but so effective. He was reliable, with tremendous concentration, such a necessary quality when you play in

Goalkeeper Bobby Brown saves a goal attempt at the feet of Dunfermline player Wright, September 1951.

Goalkeeper Bobby Brown's Scotland jersey.

goal for a Gers side that does most of the attacking in a match. Agile, with quick reflexes and totally calm, he was the ideal last line of defence behind the 'Iron Curtain'. He may only have played three times for his country, but he actually managed Scotland for 27 games.

Near the end of his time at Ibrox, he discovered how ruthless a manager Bill Struth could be. At the start of the 1952–53 season, the opening-day match saw Rangers playing Hearts at Tynecastle in the League Cup. Brown had the proverbial nightmare between the sticks as Rangers crashed to a 5–0 defeat. It was probably his worst performance in a Rangers shirt. Despite his years of brilliant displays for the side, Struth promptly dropped him in favour of George Niven, and Brown did not play another game that season. Niven started off in goal the following season, but Brown ended up replacing him for the last two thirds of it. By the next season, however, Niven had established himself as Rangers' first choice 'keeper, and by the end of the 1955–56 season Brown retired.

Having played 323 games for the club, Brown won three League Championships, three Scottish Cups and two League Cups.

## Johnny Hubbard (1949–59)

For older Rangers fans who saw him play, the name Johnny Hubbard brings back great memories of one of the game's under-rated skills – penalty taking. Hubbard was, and still is, the Ibrox penalty king. He scored an incredible 54 penalties from 57 attempts, and from 1949 until 1956 he scored with 23 consecutive kicks until Walker of Airdrie foiled him with a great save. Hubbard would be just the sort of player that modern teams could profit from when it comes to those dreaded penalty shoot-outs.

Born in Pretoria, South Africa, Hubbard arrived at Ibrox in 1949 by a rather unusual route. Willie Allison, in those days a Sunday newspaper sports editor, and later to become Gers' PR officer, received a letter from an ex-Hibs player living in South Africa. He was touted as the best player in that country and seemingly wanted to play for Rangers, and Rangers only. Allison duly informed Bill Struth, the Rangers manager, who put great faith in the recommendation and the youngster was sent for.

When he arrived at Ibrox, he probably was not what the hierarchy at Ibrox was expecting. At 5ft 4in and weighing around 8st 10lb, he did not stand out as a recruit who might excel in the tough Scottish League. His obvious homesickness and apprehensive look, coupled with his skinny build, did not produce a sense of optimism by the management. However, Struth was not the sort of man to judge on appearances, and he immediately gave Hubbard a chance to impress.

The youngster was given a tracksuit and told to meet Struth on the Ibrox pitch. When he duly appeared Struth told him to take some corner-kicks. The crosses he put over made the watchers realise that here was a player who had skill indeed. Next he was told to run towards the manager while keeping the ball up with his head. This he performed like a ball juggler in a circus. The manager was impressed by the various routines he performed as he could see that here was a youngster who had balance, ball control and was an elegant athlete. Struth took him up to his office and immediately signed him.

Johnny Hubbard would go on to become a great favourite of the Rangers fans in his 10-year stint at Ibrox. A tricky winger is always a crowd pleaser and Hubbard was that and more. His shooting prowess resulted in many spectacular goals, while his timing, great balance and dribbling ability created many more. Despite his frail-looking appearance, his bravery and ability combined to out-fox more muscular and weighty opponents throughout his career.

In the latter part of his Ibrox career, he played and scored in Rangers' first-ever European Cup tie, against OGC Nice in 1956 in France, by scoring with a penalty – what else? He also earned one cap for his native country, ironically, against his adopted one.

In April 1959 he was transferred to Bury for £6,000. The money Gers received was a bonus after the years of great service from a man who cost them nothing but the price of his trip from South Africa.

Hubbard played 258 games and scored 116 goals. He won three League Championships and one Scottish Cup.

## Billy Simpson (1950–59)

Big Ulsterman Billy Simpson's career at Ibrox spanned more or less the same years as Johnny Hubbard's. Although best known as a centre-forward, he played almost half his games as an inside-right or inside-left. He was playing with Linfield when Gers had been alerted to his ability, and Bill Struth sent former Gers star Torry Gillick over to Belfast to check the player out. Everyone knew that if the legendary Gillick was impressed then the boy must be a player. Impressed he was, and Linfield duly received a fee of £11,500 for the forward in October 1950 – then a club record.

Although a strong, brave, bustling type of centre-forward, Simpson was not the huge, brutal type prevalent in those days. His play may have lacked polish, but his bravery and eye for a goal made him that priceless commodity – a natural goalscorer. He pounced on half-chances, and his courage frequently put him in danger, especially when trying to score with diving headers, which became his speciality in the eyes of the fans with whom he built a great rapport.

Simpson became one of the few post-war Rangers to score over 100 League goals, and his 100th League goal came in October 1957 – with a flying header, of course. On three occasions he scored four goals in a match. The 1956–57 season was his greatest in terms of scoring goals, netting a total of 32. By the end of his career he had played 12 times for Northern Ireland.

Billy left Ibrox at the same time as Johnny Hubbard in 1959, but instead of going to England he went to Stirling. He remains one of the select few from Ulster to be elected to the Hall of Fame.

Simpson played 239 games and scored 163 goals. He won three League Championships and one Scottish Cup.

## Eric Caldow (1953–66)

Caldow was one of the great Rangers captains who also skippered the Scotland side, playing 40 times for his country in total. The fascinating aspect of his career is that it spanned two completely different footballing eras. When he started at Ibrox, he was joining such Rangers greats as Waddell, Woodburn and Young, but by the end of his career he was the father figure to the likes of Baxter, Henderson and Willie Johnston. Football styles had also changed from the 1950s to the 1960s and Caldow seemed at ease in both eras. Altogether he played 407 games for the club and scored 25 goals.

As a left-back, Eric Caldow was an intelligent, 'cultured' defender as opposed to a 'hard man' type. His tremendous speed, awareness and positioning made it very difficult for even the best wingers to get past him, as Real Madrid's legendary Ghento admitted after having played against him. Although only 5ft 8in and 11st, Caldow was a resilient player whose balance and compact frame increased his effectiveness. His intuition and timing in the tackle were more integral to his style than tough tackling. He was brilliant at manoeuvring opponents away from the danger areas without even resorting to a tackle unless it was necessary.

Rangers versus Eintracht Frankfurt May 1960. Eric Caldow watches as goalkeeper George Niven makes a one-handed save from Stein, European Cup semi-final at Ibrox Park, Glasgow.

Another beneficial facet to his game was his temperament. A cool, calm, dignified player, he was ideal captain material. He never lost his temper, no matter what the provocation, and never seemed to have a hair out of place at the end of a game. He truly led his side by example. Throughout his long career he was never booked – a remarkable feat for a defender!

Between 1957–63, Caldow only missed two of Scotland's games while amassing his 40 caps. His tragedy was that he looked certain to overtake George Young's number of record caps for a Rangers player when his career was virtually brought to a halt. In the 1963 Wembley match that Scotland ultimately won, Caldow suffered a leg break when he was tackled by England's bruiser of a centre-forward, Bobby Smith. In fact, his leg had been broken in three places! In those days, a broken leg was just about the most serious injury that a footballer could suffer, and thus it proved with Caldow. After a long spell out, he never really regained his form or his position in the Rangers defence and was transferred in 1966. He is now, deservedly, in Rangers' Hall of Fame.

Eric Caldow won five League Championships, two Scottish Cups and three League Cups.

## Ralph Brand (1954–65)

An Edinburgh schoolboy, Brand was spotted by Bill Struth when playing for the Scottish Schoolboys side against England at Wembley in 1952. By 1954 he had been signed by Rangers, a few months before Jimmy Millar joined the club, but it was not until the 1960–61 season that this famous striking partnership started to play together regularly. Many fans still claim that this pairing was Gers' greatest-ever partnership up front. Perhaps this came about because the two could not have been more different mentally, physically or in style. Both individually were good at their jobs, but they also complemented each other perfectly, and the 'M and B' pairing became the scourge of defences in the early 1960s.

Whereas Millar was stocky and sturdy, Brand was lean, slight and very, very quick. His electric pace could keep him out of harm's way. He was sharp, fast and brave, with a striker's instincts. An added ingredient in Brand's play was his mentality. He was a deep thinker about the game and years ahead of his time in terms of diet and taking care of his fitness. He knew that the repetitive lapping of a track in training was not the best way to prepare for games, and he voluntarily went back at the end of training to practise further and eventually roped Jimmy Millar in with him to rehearse moves and strategies. Their renowned understanding stemmed from all this practice. Even on their shared train journey from Edinburgh every morning to Ibrox, it was an opportunity for the two to discuss the game and their roles in it.

Like all great strikers, Brand had a great self-confidence and faith in his own ability, as well as the necessary mental toughness to succeed. It was these qualities that could see him through the occasional goal drought that all strikers occasionally suffer from. Also, bravery is another indispensable quality that all great strikers must have. His courage can be seen in the various injuries that he suffered through the years, including broken wrists, cracked ribs and concussion,

Ralph Brand, 1964.

to name a few. A meagre eight caps for Scotland can be explained by such injuries but more so to the presence of the legendary Denis Law who was in possession of the number-10 shirt at that time.

Considering his prolific scoring exploits, it is strange that Brand was never a top favourite with the Rangers fans – even when you consider his tally of goals against Celtic reached double figures. Probably the fans underestimated his prowess, thinking of him as merely a 'poacher'. Yet, this disparaging term is itself misleading. It implies that all a goalscorer has to do is stand around and wait for an easy chance to be tapped into the net. It ignores the ability to drift into the right place at the right time, the quick spurt of pace to get away from your marker, the alertness, anticipation and bravery necessary for all brilliant 'poaching' strikers.

A fit Ralph Brand was indeed a goalscoring machine. In the period from 1960–64, he scored a total of 147 goals in all competitions. Proof of his resilience can be seen in the fact that during this time, out of a possible 136 League appearances, Brand managed to take part in 130. In his final season, 1964–65, he only managed 17 League appearances but even then played against World Champions Inter Milan in the European Cup quarter-final in the San Siro. His last winners' medal came in that season when he helped the side defeat Celtic in the League Cup Final. At the start of the following season, he was transferred to Manchester City for £30,000 at the ridiculously young age of 28. It could justifiably be claimed that if Rangers had not let him go then, he might have scored the goals that, a couple of years later, would have changed the results of the infamous Berwick Cup loss and the defeat by Bayern in the 1967 European Cup-Winners' Cup Final.

Ralph Brand played 317 games for the club, scoring 206 goals and winning four League Championships, three Scottish Cups and four League Cups.

## Alex Scott (1954–63)

Rangers have always been famous for producing brilliant wingers, and teenage ones at that. Scott deserves to be considered one of the best in the club's history. Rangers' wingers have ranged from the fast and strong to the 'tanner ba' players. Alex Scott was the former kind – a fast and powerful winger in the mould of Willie Waddell, whom he replaced as a teenager. Indeed, in his first match for Rangers at Ibrox in 1955 he scored a hat-trick and was viewed as something of a wonderkid. To displace Waddell, who was still occasionally turning out for the club, was quite a feat.

Scott was a direct attacker who had an ability to score goals as well as create them. This was usually done by sheer speed and strength, allied with a powerful shot. As with all great wingers, Scott was a very brave player. You have to be when your job is to take on defenders, knowing that some will try to stop you at any cost. Such a thing happened in a European Cup match away to Anderlecht in 1960. In a bruising and ill-tempered encounter Scott was subjected to some very rough treatment. In the course of it he was sent flying into a boundary wall and had to go off the field for treatment. His courage was demonstrated when he returned to play on, his cut stitched up and his head swathed in bandages. There were no substitutes in those days! Despite such incidents, Scott seemed to enjoy playing against the Continentals. His finest game was probably against Borussia Mönchengladbach when Gers won 3–0 in Germany, with Scott scoring a brilliant goal from 15 yards after having dribbled past four defenders. In fact, with a tally of 12 goals, until the arrival of Ally McCoist he remained Rangers' top scorer in European matches for over 35 years.

In 1961 he was at his peak and was first choice for both Rangers and Scotland, but then another young Gers winger appeared on the scene – Willie Henderson. Although only 18, Henderson quickly challenged Scott for supremacy at Ibrox and for the international side, despite the fact that he was 6in shorter and considerably lighter. This led to some unusual and awkward situations as the players did not get on and did not speak to each other, Henderson believing that Scott was part of an older clique at Ibrox. In April 1962, Scott was dropped by Rangers in favour of

Photograph © Action Images / MSI

Rangers versus Eintracht Frankfurt, May 1960. Alex Scott has his shot deflected past the Frankfurt goalkeeper Loy in the European Cup semi-final at Ibrox Park, Glasgow.

Henderson, but it was Scott who played against England at Hampden in Scotland's first win against the Auld Enemy in 25 years. Seven days later, however, it was Henderson who played at Hampden in the Scottish Cup Final against St Mirren, picking up his first medal in a 2–0 win.

During Rangers' famous tour of Russia in 1962 the Scott–Henderson situation came to a head. When Scott had been substituted by manager Symon, allowing Henderson to go on and produce a great display, Scott had a real argument with Symon and it was reported by the Scottish journalists who were present. That was when the feud became public knowledge. The writing was on the wall for the older winger. In February 1963, he was transferred to Everton for £46,000. Although he left what was to become one of Rangers greatest-ever teams, he did have the consolation of winning an English League title and an FA Cup-winners' medal while with the Goodison club. He even played on the left wing for Scotland with his nemesis, Henderson, on the right wing. By the end of his career he had played for Scotland 16 times.

Scott played 347 games and scored 117 goals. He won four League Championships, one Scottish Cup and two League Cups.

# Chapter Three

# Players Elected
# Between 1954–67

## History of the Period

The season after the departure of Bill Struth led to new manager Scot Symon's team finishing third as he became acquainted with the rigours of managing the giants of Scotland. Symon, a former Rangers wing-half, had virtually been chosen by Struth as his successor thanks to a promising managerial career that had seen him transform East Fife while there for six seasons before taking Preston to the English Cup Final in his only season at Deepdale.

Symon reinvigorated the club. Following a third-place finish in his initial season, he guided Rangers to three Championships out of four. His team came second in that spell in the 1957–58 season, only being kept from the title by the greatest Hearts side in that club's history. With stars such as Dave McKay, Alex Young and Willie Bauld, the Tynecastle team only lost one League game and accrued an amazing 62 points out of a possible 68, scoring 132 goals in 34 matches. Still, coming behind such a fine Hearts side was not the worst aspect of that season. That came in October 1957, when Celtic beat Rangers 7–1 in the League Cup Final at Hampden, to this day the worst defeat suffered by Gers at the hands of their greatest rival.

In the meantime, Symon was letting many of the 'old guard' go while signing younger players, many of whom would go on to make their indelible mark on the club forever. Among those he signed in the 1950s were such great names as: Don Kichenbrand, Max Murray, Jimmy Millar, Alex Scott, Davie Wilson, Ian McMillan, Bobby Shearer and Eric Caldow.

It was Symon who was in charge to see another milestone in the club's history with the emergence of European football. On 24 October 1956, Rangers' first-ever European Cup game took place at Ibrox against French champions, Nice. A crowd of 65,000 watched the home side win 2–1. It took a third match at a 'neutral' venue, Paris, before the French, somewhat luckily, overcame the Scottish champions.

Rangers' next foray into Europe was slightly more successful the next season. This time the French champions, St Etienne, were dispatched in the first round before the mighty AC Milan proved to be far too good for Rangers to handle. By the 1959–60 season, however, Rangers seemed to have got the hang of the European lark and even managed to reach the semi-final.

Belgian aces Anderlecht were routed 7–2 on aggregate, followed by Czechs Red Star Bratislava 5–4 before a third game at a neutral venue – Highbury, this time – saw Rangers dismiss Dutch champions Sparta Rotterdam. The last four standing were reigning holders Real Madrid, Fairs Cup (now UEFA Cup) holders Barcelona and the German team Eintracht Frankfurt. When Rangers pulled the Germans out of the hat, the Final, at Hampden too, seemed within reach. It was an illusion. The Germans were far too skilful and sophisticated for Rangers, running out 12–4 winners on aggregate; however, even this very good German side could not live with the legendary Real, who cuffed them 7–3 in the Final. A lot would have to be learned if Europe was to be conquered.

If the 1950s ended disappointingly in Europe and domestically, with a third place in the League, then the early 1960s would usher in a tremendous period for the club. For the meantime, Rangers would have to be content with the Scottish Cup won in 1960 by beating a very good Kilmarnock side, managed, ironically, by Willie Waddell.

The early 1960s produced a golden era for Rangers and one of its greatest-ever sides. Scot Symon was at the peak of his powers and had created a team that would become Britain's first European finalists as well as win the domestic treble, the double and three League Championships in four seasons. This side probably reached its peak in 1963; although it was a year later that the treble was won with a marginally less talented team. The Rangers squad that completed the treble was: Ritchie, Shearer, Provan, Greig, McKinnon, Baxter, Henderson, McLean, Millar, Forrest, Brand, Wilson, McMillan, Watson, Willoughby. In that season of the clean sweep, young Jim Forrest, gradually taking over from legend Jimmy Millar, actually scored an incredible 56 competitive goals!

At the start of the decade the 'normal' Rangers team was: Niven; Shearer, Caldow; Davis, Paterson, Baxter; Scott, McMillan, Millar, Brand and Wilson. This was soon transformed into the formation that can still be recited by Gers fans of that era, even today, without thinking: Ritchie, Shearer, Caldow; Greig, McKinnon, Baxter; Henderson, McMillan, Millar, Brand and Wilson.

This team had everything: a great defence, two creative midfield men, two exciting wingers and a striking partnership that has never been bettered by any pairing in a Rangers shirt. In the 1962–63 season, the team won the title, only losing twice while scoring 94 goals in 34 matches. Rangers won the League Championship in three of the first four seasons of this period, only coming second to the greatest Dundee side in its history. The Scottish Cup was won on three consecutive occasions and, to add icing to the cake, Celtic were totally dominated in their encounters with Rangers. While Rangers' old rivals were languishing, Jim Baxter was strutting his stuff at Ibrox and giving the Gers fans the time of their lives.

Rangers became the first British club to contest a European Final when it reached the European Cup-Winners' Cup Final of 1961. Having disposed of Ferencvaros of Hungary, Borussia Mönchengladbach of Germany and Wolves of England en route to the two-leg Final, it was unfortunate that their opponents were Fiorentina of Italy. The ruthless, organised and skilful Italians were just too much of a handful for the Ibrox men and took the trophy by winning 2–0 at Ibrox and 2–1 in Florence.

In 1967, a second chance to lift this trophy was given to Rangers, but once again they were foiled by a superior side. This time it was the Bayern Munich side of Beckenbauer et al, who would go on to become the best team in Europe in the early 1970s. Despite the disadvantage of having to play the Germans in Nuremberg in the Final with a make-shift strike force, Rangers managed to take the match into extra-time before going down 1–0. It was all the more disappointing because a week previously Celtic had won the European Cup, and a Rangers victory would have made it the first time that the two big European trophies had been won by teams from the same city in the same season. On their way to that Final, the team had overcome: Glentoran from Northern Ireland; German side, Borussia Dortmund; Zaragoza from Spain; and Bulgars, Slavia Sofia.

As with everything else in life, all good football things must come to an end and they did – abruptly, at Ibrox, with the arrival of Jock Stein at Celtic Park. Once Stein had turned around the 'sleeping giant' of Celtic, the job of succeeding Gers' managers was going to be made doubly difficult. The Kilmarnock League title of the 1964–65 season, when Rangers finished an unacceptable fifth in the table, was the watershed for the club. Part of the reason for that disastrous League standing was obviously injuries to key players, especially Baxter and Henderson who missed more than half that season. In fact, Baxter was transferred to Sunderland at the end of the season. After that campaign, Stein's Celtic would go on to win nine consecutive League titles, with Rangers coming second no fewer than six times.

## MANAGER: SCOT SYMON (1954–1967)

When he was appointed, James Scotland Symon became only the third manager in the 80-odd-year history of Rangers. Born in Perthshire, he had already been imbued with Rangers' ethos, having played at left-half for the club after joining from Portsmouth in 1938. As a determined, brave and classy player throughout his nine years at Ibrox, he became a favourite of Bill Struth who probably recognised qualities in him that would lead to him becoming a very good manager after his playing days were over.

When he became the manager of East Fife at the age of 35, he immediately transformed the fortunes of that club. In his first season, he gained promotion for the Fifers to the top division. After that first season playing with the big boys, Symon's side had finished fourth in the table behind the champions, Rangers. It was quite an achievement!

In his six seasons at Methil, Symon worked wonders and gave the fans some precious memories. His greatest achievement was no doubt winning the League Cup, having knocked out Rangers in the semi-final. A few months later, his team played Rangers in the Scottish Cup Final but lost out to a Gers side intent on avenging its earlier shock defeat. It was inevitable that a bigger club would covet the manager, and Preston North End installed him to rejuvenate their club. In his only season at Deepdale, he took Preston to an English Cup Final at Wembley, but by then Ibrox was calling him.

His old club needed him with the departure of the ailing Bill Struth. Indeed, he was practically hand-picked by Struth to be his successor. The Grand Old Man of Ibrox obviously wanted to ensure that the new man would continue with the traditions and successes that he had established over the previous 34 years. Struth said of Symon: 'He is a man of indomitable courage, of unbreakable devotion to a purpose, a man, indeed, who became a true Ranger.' Few doubted that this man, reared in the Struth Ibrox tradition, would fail his mentor.

In fact, under Symon things continued as normal at Ibrox. He was truly a Struth apostle and did things the way they had always been done. While the trainers such as Davie Kinnear worked with the players, Symon would stand on the sidelines, occasionally shouting instructions. Standing there in his hat and coat, he was to be one of the last of the 'old school' managers. His methods worked throughout the 1950s and early 1960s, but then a new type of manager was being seen more frequently – the 'track suit manager'. Unfortunately, one particular 'track suit manager' was Symon's immediate opponent Jock Stein, who would revolutionise Celtic, making them the top dogs in Scotland well past Symon's sacking.

Like Struth before him, Symon knew a player when he saw one and understood how that player should fit into his side. He believed that the main part of his job was to identify quality players, acquire them for the club and blend them with the other quality stars he had already. This policy bore spectacular fruits when the Rangers side of 1960–63 was at its peak. Many older Gers fans still believe that this side was Rangers' greatest ever.

Again, like Struth, Symon was not a man of tactics. He left his players on the field to decide how the team should play, how they should deal with the opposition as the match unfolded. His job was not to coach them or lay down tactics but to form a team pattern and supply the players whose quality would overcome their opponents. This he did admirably – until the arrival of Stein at Celtic.

Scot Symon was the opposite of Stein. Symon was a quiet, dignified, honest, seemingly rather aloof type of individual who kept his distance from his players and, crucially, the media. In his business suit, he looked every inch the middle-class 'perfect gentleman' that his players respected. Meanwhile, at Celtic Park, a track-suited Jock Stein was coaching his players on the training ground and learning about modern tactics by visiting the training complexes of such foreign coaches as Herrera at Inter Milan. A working-class hero in the making, Big Jock would be lionised by the football press and become as much a star as any of his players. The emergence of Stein and the ageing of the team of the first half of the 1960s, in addition to the departure of Baxter, combined eventually to lead to Symon's downfall at Ibrox.

Despite having beaten Celtic in the 1966 Scottish Cup Final, by 1967 Symon's teams were struggling to keep up with Celtic in the League. The writing was perhaps on the wall when the greatest shock defeat in Rangers' history occurred in January of that year. Little Rangers, Berwick, knocked their more famous namesakes out of the Scottish Cup in the first round. The entire country was stunned but nobody more so than Scot Symon. He said that this defeat was 'the worst result in the club's history'. Rangers' two strikers that day, Jim Forrest and George McLean, for failing to at least equal the solitary Berwick goal, were made the scapegoats and told they would never play for the club again. They were later transferred to other clubs. Both, especially Forrest, were young men, not even in their prime and so the decision to get rid of them was undoubtedly wrong, but it is believed that there was pressure from the board to take this course of action in order to emphasise just how humiliating the Berwick defeat had been for the directors as well as everybody else at the club.

This particular decision came back to haunt Symon and Rangers a few months later. Despite a poor showing in the Scottish Cup, Rangers had been progressing well in the European Cup-Winners' Cup and actually made it to the Final in May 1967. Unfortunately, this led to an even bigger disappointment than the Berwick debacle. It should not have been a surprise, however, as the odds had seemed stacked against Rangers from the start. They were playing Bayern Munich, about to become one of the top clubs in Europe. They were virtually playing them at home, in Nuremberg to be exact. They were playing them only a week after Stein's Celtic had become the first British club to lift the European Cup, adding to the pressure the club was under to be successful. What is more, having got rid of their two top strikers earlier in the season, Rangers were forced to play a centre-half, Roger Hynd, at centre-forward – and against the great Franz Beckenbauer at that!

Despite all these handicaps, Rangers took the Final into extra-time before a solitary strike saw the Germans lift the trophy. It was to be another five years before Rangers got their hands on that Cup. Afterwards, thinking back on one glaring miss by temporary striker Hynd, chairman John Lawrence stretched out his hands and claimed that, but for that distance, he might have been awarded a knighthood in a similar fashion to Celtic's Sir Bob Kelly after his club's Lisbon triumph.

If that result cost Lawrence a knighthood, then, ultimately it would cost Symon his job. After Nuremberg, it was recognised that new training methods and tactics would be required at Ibrox, so bright newcomer to management, Davie White, the Clyde manager, was hired to 'assist' Symon. It was obvious that White was being groomed to be Symon's successor, but nobody could have guessed just how soon!

The following season, Symon used the money furnished by the board to buy new blood for his team. Players such as Alex Ferguson, Orjan Persson and Eric Sorensen arrived but were limited successes. Ironically, when the axe fell on Symon, in November, Rangers were top of the table and looking a better side than the previous season's one. When the board terminated his contract, few Rangers fans objected to the action but they did query the way that it had been done. Instead of a face-to-face meeting, John Lawrence sent a businessman friend to speak to Symon at the businessman's home, indicating the board's wishes. The dignified yet appalled Symon felt betrayed and the majority of fans felt that a loyal club servant had been shabbily treated. Symon did not even get the chance to clear out his desk, let alone say his goodbyes to the players. The only times he ever visited Ibrox from then on were in his capacity as Partick Thistle manager. Symon's dismissal was not one of Rangers' finest hours.

# Players Elected

## Billy Ritchie (1955–67)

Billy Ritchie took over from another good Rangers 'keeper in George Niven, and his career spanned the 1950s and 1960s, making him one of the last of the old style 'keepers who believed in being efficient, focussed and unspectacular. Born in Newtongrange, he was a Hearts supporter when he joined Rangers at the age of 17. As a youngster, he had started playing football as a left-back, then a left-winger before trying goalkeeping by accident. His amateur team had found themselves a man short and so Billy went in goal – and never looked back.

By the time he had become more than a competent 'keeper, in 1955, Arsenal, Everton and Aston Villa wanted to sign him, but he had already agreed to go to Ibrox and kept his word to Rangers. Only the brilliance of George Niven and having to do his stint of National Service in the Army kept him out of the Rangers side

Photograph © Action Images / MSI

Goalkeeper Billy Ritchie saves a shot from Kurt Hamrin at Ibrox Park, Glasgow, during the European Cup-Winners' Cup Final first leg against Fiorentina, May 1961.

initially. Ritchie was an efficient, hard-working, dedicated and ever-so-reliable 'keeper who only performed the spectacular when he had to. He excelled in reading of the game, proper positioning and anticipation – all features of goalkeeping that made him a great shot-stopper. Without being a giant, he was more than capable at dealing with crosses and was never a goalline type of 'keeper.

In those days at Ibrox, as with most clubs, the 'keepers trained in the same way as the out-field players by running and doing the various exercises. Ritchie, however, was ahead of his time in that he voluntarily, off his own bat, went to the gym and worked out after 'normal' training before doing some specific goalkeeping training with reserve 'keeper Norrie Martin.

Most older fans who saw him credited Ritchie with playing a big part in Rangers getting to the first Final of the European Cup-Winners' Cup in 1960, especially by making a 'wonder' save in the semi-final away to Wolves when he somehow saved a 30-yard thunderbolt from England player Ron Flowers. Sometimes he did do the spectacular! The fact that he only won one Scotland cap can probably be attributed to the fact that the brilliant Bill Brown of Spurs held the international jersey for a number of years. Ironically, when he left Ibrox, he followed in the footsteps of his predecessor Niven by joining Partick Thistle.

Ritchie played 340 games and had 120 shut-outs. He won two League Championships, four Scottish Cups (including the very rare three consecutive ones) and three League Cups.

## Bobby Shearer (1955–65)

When Shearer joined Rangers in 1955 from his home-town team of Hamilton for £2,000 it should have been obvious that he was a Rangers captain in the making. Right from the start, he was imbued with the 'Rangers spirit' and no wonder as he found himself under the tutelage of such legends as George Young, Sammy Cox and Willie Waddell, who were all coming to the end of their Rangers careers.

Shearer, at right-back, was a complete contrast to his full-back partner on the left, Eric Caldow. While Caldow was very fast and 'cultured', Shearer was dour, gritty and determined with that invaluable never-say-die spirit. He was a robust but fair tackler and must have terrified some of his opponents at times. He always showed great bravery, and his sense of anticipation, positional sense and timing in the tackle meant that few attackers got past him easily. His nickname, 'Captain Cutlass', says it all – he did not take prisoners when it came to a battle on the pitch.

Having said that, Shearer was never ordered off in his Gers career and never appeared in front of the dreaded Referee Committee that dealt with errant players. Incredibly, it was seven years before he conceded his first penalty – and that was for handling, in a game against Motherwell. Perhaps even more remarkably, he played 30 European games without being booked by any Continental referees, who, in those days, did not normally take kindly to the 'British-style' of tackling. He was the complete contrast to full-back partner Eric Caldow, who was fast and clever. Shearer instead relied on determination and bravery coupled with great timing in the tackle, good positioning and anticipation. For a 'hard man' he avoided injury well and even played 175 consecutive games (then about three full seasons) – almost unthinkable nowadays for a defender.

In a 1960 game against Hearts at Tynecastle, 'keeper Billy Ritchie was carried off so captain courageous, Shearer, undaunted, took over in goal and made some good saves. It was just another day at the office for Bobby. He became Rangers captain in

Photograph © Action Images / MSI

Bobby Shearer shakes hands with Danny Blanchflower of Spurs in 1962.

1962 and led the club to the treble (for only the second time) in 1963–64, which was his finest hour and proudest as a Rangers fan. After he retired, he remained a supporter of the club in the media, defending Rangers when the critics were rounding on the club for whatever reason.

Shearer played 451 games for Rangers, scoring four goals, and won five League titles, three Scottish Cups, four League Cups and four Scotland Caps.

## Jimmy Millar (1955–67)

He was not a pacey player and, at only 5ft 6in, he was not a powerful, tall, target man, but in the period between 1960–64 Millar scored over 100 goals for Rangers and made many, many more. He was simply one of the greatest Rangers centre-forwards of all time. He joined the club in 1955 from Dunfermline for a fee of £5,000, having turned down the chance to join Preston. His early mentors were greats such as Waddell, Young, Cox and McColl, and this former Hearts-daft lad learned the ways of Rangers from them.

Millar was sturdily built, and it took quite a thwack to barge him off the ball. He was not averse to doing a bit of barging himself either, as most strikers did in those days. Perhaps because he had been converted from being a wing-half, he was a better passer of the ball than most strikers and led the forward line well, linking up with his fellow forwards brilliantly. He could also score goals with both feet and with his head. Considering his lack of height, he was a real handful in the air for most defenders and had the ability to climb above them as if sheer determination alone could outdo them.

One of his most obvious virtues was his bravery and will-to-win. He had that traditional Rangers never-say-die spirit. He even helped Gers defeat Celtic in the 1963 Ne'er Day game, despite the fact that he had had to get out of his sick bed, suffering from flu, and catch the train from Edinburgh to join up with his teammates. Such dedication and spirit is invaluable to any side. Millar had the biggest heart around. He was never one to shirk a tackle and could give and take knocks without fear or favour. This being the case, he suffered numerous injuries throughout his career, from a broken collar bone to ligament injuries and everything in between. Unfortunately, these cost him dearly in terms of international representation and he had to withdraw from many Scotland squads. Sadly, he only played for his country twice – a gross injustice for such a fine player.

At the height of his career, Bill Shankly tried to sign him for Liverpool, but Rangers rejected the possibility without even informing the player, who only learned about the possible move years later from Shankly himself. He never regretted staying with the club, though, and won many domestic honours as a reward. In the early 1960s, Millar formed a deadly and legendary striking partnership with fellow Edinburgh man, Ralph Brand. What became known to the fans as 'M and B' devastated many a defence, thanks to the understanding that the pair developed over the years. Brand was light years ahead of most fellow professionals in those days and was a deep thinker about the game, its tactics and methods. He encouraged Millar to join him in extra training sessions after most of the others had gone home in order to develop moves to outfox defences. How it paid off! The quick, lithe Brand was the ideal foil for Millar and vice-versa.

During the latter part of his Ibrox career, Millar experimented with a deeper-lying role as centre-forward, and the extra space enabled him to continue scoring and making many more goals. By the 1965–66 season, Millar was coming to the end of his Rangers career, with the brilliant young Jim Forrest taking over at centre-forward. Still, Jimmy had his moments of glory – none more so than when he played in his old position of wing-half in the Old Firm Scottish Cup Final replay of

Jimmy Millar, 1964.

Photograph © Action Images / MSI

1966, won by that famous Kai Johansen goal. That night it was Millar who best exemplified the spirit that took the side to victory against a superior team.

In 1967, Millar was transferred to Dundee United. Ironically, one of the young United players who could not hide his admiration for his goalscoring hero, even at this veteran stage, was a certain Walter Smith, who would become Rangers' manager in 20-odd years' time.

Jimmy Millar played 317 times for Rangers. He scored 160 goals, won three League Championships, five Scottish Cups and three League Cups.

## Harold Davis (1956–64)

Unlike Clint Eastwood, nobody would ever have called this Ranger 'Dirty Harry'. He was tough and uncompromising, the sort of guy who would have eaten Vinnie Jones for breakfast, but he was always the gentleman. In the fans' parlance of the time Harold was the team's 'iron man'. His teammates gave him the nickname 'Hoss' after the gentle giant with the inner steel who was a character in the popular cowboy TV series *Bonanza*. Davis would have been Jock Wallace's ideal player, and there would have been a mutual respect between these two ex-Army men. Jock might have done his duty in Malaya, but Harry Davis had seen action during the Korean War. Indeed, Davis had been wounded in action, so a kick or two from an opposing forward amounted to nothing when compared to the trials of combat.

The big Fifer was signed by Rangers from East Fife in October 1956. His Ibrox career actually spanned two eras. When he first appeared in the team he found himself alongside legends such as George Young and Ian McColl, but in the later stages of his spell at Ibrox he was playing with Jim Baxter and Willie Henderson in the great side of the early 1960s. One well-known funny story that perhaps sums up Harry Davis happened when Harry took exception to something said by jester-in-chief Baxter. During a game, Baxter had given Davis 'pelters', as they used to say, when he had twice tried to be fancy and lost possession – not something that Jim Baxter would ever have done, of course. Being 'fancy' was not Harold's forte. Afterwards, in the dressing room, Harold took Baxter to task for insulting him. He grabbed him, lifted him off the ground and told him in no uncertain terms that if he ever spoke to him again like that he would kill him. Further confrontation was avoided when manager Scot Symon appeared and shouted across the dressing room, 'Put Jim down, Harold, put Jim down!'

Nobody messed with Harold. He was the type of player that every great team needs. He was a grafter, the man with the heart and the bite to allow the skilful ball-players the freedom to do their own thing, knowing that Harold would mop up any mistakes. The man from the Kingdom of Fife had that never-say-die spirit that Rangers teams have exemplified from the time of the club's foundation. Davis was ready to play until he dropped. He genuinely believed that the club was more important than the individual – that a real Rangers player cared more for the club's dignity and honour than his own personal glorification.

Since he was not blessed with natural pace, Davis compensated with a great sense of positioning and anticipation. As for his tackling ability – he would have tackled a tank, as he probably had in Korea. When Rangers played a second leg Cup-Winners' Cup tie in Seville in 1962, the Spaniards got so violent and out of control that the match became infamous as 'The Battle of Seville'. Various Gers players were butted, kicked, punched and even bitten – but Harry Davis was not one of them!

Perhaps the incident involving Davis that is most fondly remembered by older Gers fans came in a European Cup tie at Ibrox against Belgian champions Anderlecht in 1960. Rangers, in front of 80,000 fans, eventually won the first leg 5–2 but not before the Belgians had tried to intimidate them using every Continental trick in the book – and some that were not. The Anderlecht players completely lost the plot, indulging in all kinds of tripping, pushing and body-checking in an effort to stop the Ibrox side. Afterwards, their officials even admitted to feeling ashamed of their players' conduct.

At one point, the Anderlecht forward Joseph Jurion provided the final straw – as far as Harold was concerned. This player actually wore glasses while playing. Still, he must have been very short-sighted to have had the nerve to take on Davis. After the ball had been cleared, Davis was sent crashing to the ground. But then Jurion kicked Harold while he was lying on the ground. Davis was a fair player and a gentleman, but he could take no more. As Davis staggered to his feet, Jurion could see the look on Harry's face and, terrified, he decided that discretion was the better part of valour. He legged it! The astonished crowd was treated to the sight of one scared Belgian being chased halfway up the park by one enraged Scotsman. Thanks to his sense of injustice, Davis, not known for his pace, covered the ground like Linford Christie. Fortunately for his opponent, just as Harry caught up with him, he saw the absurd side to the whole affair, pulled up and burst out laughing. What the Belgian burst out with was never recorded. The lucky man must have been one of the few players to have messed with Harold Davis and get away with it – sort of!

Davis played 261 games and scored 13 goals. He won four League Championships, one Scottish Cup and two League Cups.

## Davie Wilson (1956–67)

As this book hopefully has already shown, Rangers has always been a club where tremendous wingers have thrived, from Alan Morton and Willie Waddell to Willie Henderson and beyond. Davie Wilson was Rangers' left-winger after Johnny Hubbard and before Willie Johnston. He was better than both of those and arguably Gers' best-ever left-winger, apart from Alan Morton, Davie Cooper and Brian Laudrup.

Photograph © Action Images / MSI

Davie Wilson in the May 1963 Scottish Cup Final at Hampden Park, Glasgow, with McNamee of Celtic rushing in to tackle.

At 5ft 6in tall he was 'normal' size for 1960s wingers and 2in taller than Willie Henderson playing on the opposite wing. Despite his fragile-looking frame, the fair-haired Wilson had an inner steel about him and could take the numerous knocks that any winger is liable to suffer, simply getting up after having been pole-axed and getting on with it. He was fortunate in that during his best years at Ibrox he always had another great winger on the right to help relieve the pressure on him to create chances. First it was the powerful Alex Scott, to be followed by the tricky Willie Henderson. Still, Wilson did create many chances and, even more so than his fellow wingers, scored goals too.

While Henderson was causing havoc on the right, opening up defences, Millar and Brand would be keeping the defenders in the middle busy which would allow Wilson to ghost in from the left and pounce on any opportunities that came his way. His job was also made easier by having the rest of his left flank graced by Eric Caldow at full-back and the peerless Jim Baxter feeding passes through to him.

In style, Wilson was more like Alex Scott than Willie Henderson. He was not a 'tanner ba' type but was fast, direct and mentally at least one step ahead of his opponents. He could be an inspiring sight, this blond-haired winger buzzing down the left, ready to fling over a deadly cross or complete a one-two that would open up the goal. He was also an incredibly versatile forward, and in one spell over three seasons he actually played in every forward position. He even played at left-back successfully for club and country.

Still, for an out-and-out winger his scoring feats would take some beating. He even managed to score six goals when substituting for Millar at centre-forward in a 7–1 win at Brockville. As usual, courage, determination as well as skill were the factors that made him such a success. No wonder opposition fans detested him, as he was such a thorn in their teams' sides. It was presumably from this quarter that his nickname of 'Polaris' (the submarine) emanated, because of his propensity (as they saw it) to dive, dive, dive in the penalty area! However, Gers fans would claim that he was deservedly awarded so many penalties because foul play was the only way the opposition could stop him at times.

A Glaswegian, Wilson was a Rangers fan from his youth and joined the club at the age of 17. It was the 1959–60 season in which he became the first-choice left-winger, playing in the European Cup semi-final that season against Eintracht Frankfurt. Having said that, he had actually made his European debut in 1957 when he played in the away leg of the European Cup tie against St Etienne, marking the game by scoring a goal.

Once he had become established in the Rangers first team, Wilson soon became a Scotland fixture also. His worst and best moments playing for Scotland were probably both at Wembley. In 1961, he was in the side that went down 9–3 to England, but two years later he became a real hero in the Scots' 2–1 win over the English. Wilson's contribution was memorable for unusual reasons, however. Captain Eric Caldow had been stretchered off early on with a broken leg and, with no subs in those days, Wilson was moved to left-back as the 10-man Scots overcame all the odds to win. Wilson played the game of his life with his cool play and tenacious tackling, even annoying the English players and fans with time-wasting pass-backs etc. It was his finest hour in 22 appearances for his country.

In the heyday period between 1960–64, Wilson scored 98 goals in all competitions – a great tally for a winger. He came second only to Ralph Brand in terms of League goals scored. All this in addition to being a very dangerous winger who created so many goals for others. The event that arguably changed his career was an injury – a broken leg to be exact. This happened in a League Cup semi-final in October 1963 against Berwick Rangers and caused him to miss the 5–0 defeat of Morton in the Final. He made up for this at least by playing in the 1964 Scottish Cup Final against Dundee and picking up yet another winners' medal.

By that time, however, he was struggling to hold off the challenge from another brilliant but younger left-winger, Willie Johnston, who would even appear for Scotland in 1965. Although he eventually did lose his place, Wilson still played alongside Willie Johnston in the triumphant 1966 Scottish Cup Final replay against Celtic. Right to the end of his Ibrox career, Wilson was still scoring goals for the team. Even by 1967, he scored the only goal of the game in Rangers' away leg of the Cup-Winners' Cup semi-final against Slavia Sofia, a goal which ensured that Rangers qualified for the Final.

At the start of the following season, though, he was transferred, like Jimmy Millar, to Dundee United, still only 28 years of age. Maybe he had not been Alan Morton – but until that time he had been the next best thing!

Davie Wilson played 373 matches for Rangers, scoring 155 goals. He won two League Championships, five Scottish Cups and two League Cups.

# Davie Provan (1958–70)

Although born in Falkirk, Davie Provan had always been 'Rangers daft', so it was the proverbial dream come true when he joined the club in 1958. It was just as well because he had a long wait before he became a first-team regular. At 6ft 2in he was probably too tall and lanky to be a full-back, but Gers had signed him initially as a centre-half. With Bill Paterson and then Ronnie McKinnon ahead of him for that position, however, Provan was turned into a left-back, although he could play on the right as well. Still, this change did not lead to an immediate improvement in his first team prospects as he then found himself in the reserves for five years, understudy to the redoubtable Shearer and Caldow, waiting for either of them to be injured.

Eventually, in April 1963, Eric Caldow broke his leg playing at Wembley, and Provan's time had come. He became a reliable part of the side that was in the process of winning the double and that would go on to win the treble the following season. Unfortunately, that was the high point of his career as Rangers and Provan went downhill from then on. With Caldow's injury he was thrown in at the deep end to play in a Scottish Cup semi-final against Dundee United, followed by two games against Celtic in the first Old Firm Cup Final in 30 years – so no pressure there then. At that point he had only played in 11 matches all season, which meant that he was not eligible for a League-winners' medal, although he certainly earned the one he won the following season.

Being so tall, his long legs were an obvious advantage (similar to 'Daddy Long Legs' Manderson) when it came to tackling opponents. His height was also an advantage when it came to dealing with crosses to the back post, but equally his height was a disadvantage when it came to opposing small wingers such as Jimmy Johnstone of Celtic who was only 5ft 4in and who must have felt that he could have run between Provan's legs at times. Wingers such as this gave Provan his greatest problems. Still, he was a dogged and determined defender who showed a consistency that every defence needs. A dedicated pro and a guy who played for the jersey, he deserved his success when it eventually arrived. He fitted well into a great Rangers side but struggled rather more when the team declined. Five caps for Scotland suggest that he was more than a workman-like player. A bonus was that he could take a penalty well and was confident to stand in for the regular penalty-taker when required.

Provan played 262 games and scored 11 goals. He won one League Championship, three Scottish Cups and two League Cups.

# Willie Henderson (1960–72)

One of Rangers' most significant aspects of its style of play from its inception has been its utilisation of brilliant wingers, especially very youthful ones. Willie Henderson was such a player. At the age of 18 he was so outstanding that he found himself vying with Scottish international Alex Scott for Rangers' right-wing berth at Ibrox and also for his country. Whereas some Gers' wingers, like Scott, had relied on pace and power to get past opponents, Wee Willie, as he was affectionately called, used pace coupled with trickery. His flexibility, his talent for twisting and turning, tying his opponents seemingly in knots was the precursor for Celtic's 'Jinky' Johnstone a few years later. Henderson was the traditional Scottish 'tanner ba' player supreme, bamboozling defenders with his excellent ball control, complemented by his twisting and weaving runs that mesmerised opponents, teammates and fans alike.

Even in the early 1960s, he seemed a throwback from the good old days when such players had been the norm rather than the exception. So good was his tight control that at times it must have seemed as if he had the ball tied to his bootlaces. Perhaps this was just as well for he was so short-sighted that he had to wear contact lenses to be able to see anything at all!

Photograph © Action Images / MSI

Willie Henderson in March 1972.

As with all great wingers, Wee Willie was a brave player, always ready to take stick from frustrated defenders and come back for more. Sometimes, he seemed like the ball itself in his ability to be bounced about before getting up after persistent fouls and taking on the same defenders. Those opponents who did not know him probably thought that at only 5ft 4in tall, he would be 'easy meat'. How wrong they were! In order to even foul him, they first had to catch him. His pace, trickery, bravery and supreme confidence made most defenders' task a nightmare. Also, although small in stature, he was quite a muscular player and could use this to good effect too.

Henderson did not score as many goals as other Gers' wingers such as Scott and Wilson but he made so many more. He was a far more profitable player in terms of creating chances for his colleagues. His forte was in racing to the byline, having left umpteen opponents in his wake, before cutting the ball back low, across the face of the goal, for his strikers to run on to and crash the ball into the net. With brilliant forwards like Millar and Brand in the centre, not to mention fellow winger Davie Wilson coming in from the back post, it was no wonder that Henderson's runs resulted in so many goals.

Despite his talent for bobbing and weaving and dribbling round defenders, making them look foolish, Henderson, in the eyes of many, was a superior winger to the later Jimmy Johnstone due to the fact that Wee Willie was more direct and effective. Henderson's trickery and speed were used simply to get into a position to deliver a telling cross or cut-back. Seldom would you see him beat the same defender two or three times, a la Johnstone, with no progress having been made.

Henderson had joined the club in January 1961, despite the fact that many English clubs such as Manchester United were desperate to sign him. He only played three matches that season, but the following season was his first real spell in the team, battling with Alex Scott for his place on the wing. At 18, he made his debut for Scotland, playing against Wales in a Home International match. The 1962–63 season was probably his finest campaign, making an impact at home and abroad with Rangers as well as doing the business for Scotland. He was a vital member of the Scottish team that beat Spain 6–2 in Madrid in a friendly as well as defeating England for three consecutive seasons, eventually amassing 29 caps.

Perhaps Wee Willie's most memorable hour, however, came near the end of the classic 1964 Scottish Cup Final when Rangers beat Dundee 3–1. With the teams drawing 1–1 with only a couple of minutes left, Henderson became the Gers' hero. His devastating runs and crosses created the second goal for Jimmy Millar and the third for Ralph Brand to win the trophy. A couple of years later he added to his Scottish Cup tally of winners' medals when he took part in the famous Kai Johansen defeat of Celtic in the 1966 replay. At the age of 22, Henderson had won four Scottish Cup medals – quite an achievement!

By that stage, though, injuries were a recurring feature of his career, curtailing his appearances and performances. A bunion operation followed by strains, muscle pulls and many minor ailments seemed to hamper his progress. He soldiered on, however, and was still capable, on occasion, of producing match-winning performances or goals. Throughout his Ibrox career, he had always been an entertainer and crowd-pleaser, but as the years wore on he became less consistent – the bugbear of all wingers. He had been a valuable asset to the club, and nobody grudged his eventual move to Sheffield Wednesday in 1972.

Henderson played 426 matches for Rangers and scored 62 goals, winning two League Championships, four Scottish Cups and two League Cups.

## Ronnie McKinnon (1960–73)

In the 30-year spell from 1956 to 1986, from George Young to Terry Butcher, most Rangers fans would agree that the best centre-half the club had was Ronnie McKinnon. One of the few Govan boys to have played for Rangers, he grew up supporting the team and dreaming about playing for the Gers. He started with the Juniors, playing for Dunipace before joining the local side near Ibrox, Benburb or 'The Bens' as they were known to the natives. When he signed in 1959 it was as an inside-forward, but he played as a wing-half in the reserves at the start of his Ibrox career. With players like Jim Baxter, Harold Davis and Billy Stevenson already vying for these two positions, however, his prospects seemed remote. Rangers decided to try him out as a centre-half – and he never looked back.

At 5ft 11in tall McKinnon was not exactly the typical towering, overpowering centre-half of the time; however, while still competent in the air, thanks to a good sense of timing, he was even better on the ground. The fact that he had started out as what modern fans would call a 'midfield man' meant that McKinnon had an awareness of what was happening around him, that he had a greater mobility coupled with a composure which enabled him to make use of the ball in a more constructive way while playing it out of defence.

Photograph © Action Images / MSI

Ronnie McKinnon boots the ball out of the penalty area during a friendly European match against Moscow Torpedo, November 1962.

Ronnie was a dedicated professional who was a thoroughly reliable and efficient performer for many years. Throughout the 1960s he formed a tremendous central-defensive partnership with John Greig that was the bedrock of that side. In all, he played 28 times for Scotland, competing throughout his career with Celtic's Billy McNeill for the Scotland number-five jersey. An indication of how hard it was for various international managers to choose between the two is the fact that McNeill gained one more cap than McKinnon.

Unlike McNeill, McKinnon was not a goalscoring centre-half who could come up at corners and set pieces to score important goals. McKinnon only scored three goals for Rangers, but one in particular was vital. It happened in 1964, in Belgrade in a European Cup second-leg tie against Red Star. With Gers losing 4–1, making the aggregate score 5–4 to Red Star, McKinnon scored with a diving header in the last minute. There was no away goals rule in those days, so a replay at Highbury was the result, and Rangers went into the next round thanks to a 3–1 victory.

McKinnon's greatest tragedy was that, due to injury, he missed out on Rangers' 1972 European Cup-Winners' Cup victory in Barcelona. Earlier, in the quarter-final, second leg against Sporting Lisbon, away, he had suffered a broken leg and failed to recover in time to play in the Final. As a token of gratitude for his efforts in the earlier rounds, the club took McKinnon with it as part of the official party to Barcelona. As if missing out on Gers' greatest achievement in Europe was not bad enough, to make matters worse he had been one of the survivors of the 1967 Cup-Winners' Cup Final played in Nuremberg when Gers had lost in extra-time to Bayern Munich. It was obviously not McKinnon's lucky tournament.

McKinnon's leg break was supposed to heal in around six months, but it was so bad that it took all of 18 months to clear up. He never could get back to being the player he had been. The injury, plus the fact that the player was now at the veteran stage, effectively brought an end to his great Rangers career. McKinnon will always be remembered as a guy who played for the jersey. He was consistent, loyal, reliable and someone around whom a defence could have confidence.

He played 473 games and scored three goals, winning two League Championships, four Scottish Cups and three League Cups.

## Willie Mathieson (1960–75)

Willie Mathieson was one of those players who had to wait a long time to get his break and become a first-team regular. He had joined Rangers in 1960 when, unfortunately for him, he had the great Eric Caldow and then Davie Provan ahead of him for possession of the left-back slot. Since both these players are now in the Hall of Fame you can imagine the youngster's frustration in his early days. Another factor that decreased his chances of being given a different position in the side was the fact that he was totally one-footed, with the joke at the time being that he only used his right foot for standing on. Eventually, when he did become a Gers regular, the fans dubbed him 'Wan Fit Wullie'.

His long wait for a starting spot turned out to be worth it as he was one of the Rangers heroes who won the European Cup-Winners' Cup in Barcelona in 1972 when he was almost 30. Maybe his patience had stemmed from a natural resilience toughened by having spent two years down the pits in Fife when he had left school just before his 15th birthday. He was actually born in Cardenden and had been at the same school as that other Gers Great Willie Johnston, who was a bit younger than him but who eventually shared that Barcelona stage alongside him. When he signed for Rangers, Mathieson got a £20 signing-on fee, and it was on a two-year part-time contract as he wisely wanted to finish his apprenticeship as an electrician in the mines. Thanks to Rangers, he never did have to go back down the pits.

Scot Symon, the Gers manager, had his players at times working in groups of three at the club's Albion training ground, and Mathieson found himself teamed up with Caldow and another Gers' legend, Bobby Shearer. If he could not learn from these two tremendous full-backs then he did not deserve to be at Ibrox. Another bonus was that when he was put into the third team, he was coached by the legendary Tiger Shaw. What a brilliant football upbringing he had!

It took until 1965, however, before he made his first-team debut in a 3–0 win against Hamilton in the Scottish Cup. Sadly, this only came about because Caldow had broken his leg in 1963 and his permanent replacement, Provan, later also broke his leg, allowing the Fifer to get his chance at last. You can imagine Mathieson's feelings as he lined up behind Jim Baxter. Slim Jim told the newcomer that all he had to do was win the ball when defending, make sure that he passed it to him and let him do the rest. If only football was as easy as that nowadays! Still, that debut did not signal a regular berth in the side, and it was mainly back to the reserves for Mathieson, with the occasional outing in the first team.

It was only when Willie Waddell became Rangers manager that Mathieson became a Gers mainstay. Waddell took over the ailing club and decided to get back to Rangers' traditional basics. In Mathieson he saw a dedicated pro, a hard-working, resilient, reliable and loyal player who would always give 100 per cent for the team. Everybody knew that Mathieson was not an outstanding individual player but most could see that he was the type of player that every side needs, particularly in defence. Mathieson would never hit the heights, but he would never plumb the depths either. His grit and determination would see him take care of many, more talented, forwards in big games. His pace was also an asset when it came to matching the foreign stars in Gers' run to Barcelona in 1972. So reliable and fit was he that he played in every game of that successful Cup-Winners' Cup campaign.

Apart from Barcelona, probably his other great moment was when he played in Rangers 3–2 win in the Centenary Scottish Cup Final in 1973 against Celtic when Tom Forsyth scored his unforgettable winner. On the other hand, he was unlucky in that by the time Rangers had regained the League title after a 10-year wait he was out of the first-team picture. He left the club in 1975 on a free transfer and joined Arbroath, where he also took a part-time job as an electrician again. That decision to finish his apprenticeship all those years ago certainly paid off.

Willie Mathieson played 276 games and scored three goals. He won one European Cup-Winners' Cup and one Scottish Cup.

## Jim Baxter (1960–65)

If John Greig was rightly voted 'The Greatest Ranger' then Jim Baxter, in the eyes of most fans, could rightly also be considered as the best Ranger ever. Sir Bobby Robson called Baxter 'sheer genius', icon Denis Law stated that 'a pass from Baxter was like a guided missile' and auld enemy Liverpool's Emlyn Hughes said that he was 'a fabulous, fabulous player'. Even his friend and one-time Old Firm rival Pat Crerand claimed that Baxter's talent was 'a gift from God'. Baxter won the admiration of practically every player, manager and supporter who ever saw him in his heyday.

Jim Baxter holds up the Scottish League Cup in 1965 after Rangers had beaten Celtic 2–1.

God's gift, innate ability, natural talent – call it what you will, it was not the result of coaching or a strict training regime. After his career, Baxter confessed that his one regret was that he had not taken care of his skills by training as hard and conscientiously as he might have done. He realised, only when it was too late, that your body is your prime asset and its fitness is the foundation for everything else.

As a Fife lad, Baxter had actually supported Hibs, probably because he wanted to be different from all his pals and because the Famous Five attack of the 1950s Hibs was an exciting unit to watch. Still, even in his youth Baxter was more interested in playing football than watching it. Like most of his friends he just wanted to play every available minute of every day. Unlike most of them, however, it was clear to see that Baxter had natural ability and used it to the full when in possession of the ball. By the end of the 1959–60 season he had been so outstanding for his local team Raith Rovers that a move to Ibrox was no surprise. That season he had actually played against Rangers, scoring a goal and looking brilliant in a Rovers 3–1 win at Ibrox. When he was transferred to Rangers for £17,500 at the end of the season it was a Scottish record. The princely sum of £1,000 was his signing-on fee and, at the age of 21, he was now earning £22 basic per week, plus the win bonuses that would frequent at Ibrox in the early 1960s.

For a newcomer, Baxter stood out immediately. His self-confidence and ability meant that he became a star from his first games in a Rangers shirt. He was also lucky in that he was joining what would become, arguably, the greatest Rangers side of all time. His elegance, arrogance, vision and sublime passing skills with his left foot made him not only fit into the Gers side from the start but control it too. Baxter was the maestro, his left foot the baton, conducting an orchestra full of virtuoso performers who composed a symphony on so many memorable occasions in the early 1960s. The silky passes of Slim Jim were tailor-made for wingers like Henderson and Wilson, not to mention the route through the middle where Millar, Brand and, latterly, Jim Forrest ran on to score from defence-splitting passes.

One aspect of Baxter's image that is undeserved is that he was 'lazy'. Agreed, he did not cover every blade of grass in the Greig manner, and he did not track back and tackle or chase anything in sight, but he did not simply make a pass and then stand back and admire his handiwork. Mostly, he would move for a return pass or stride forward to get involved with the play again. In his Gers side he was not required to defend. Players such as McKinnon, Greig, Caldow and Shearer were there to do that job. Baxter's job was to create, and not only did he do that but he also did it in an entertaining way.

If Baxter's motivation was to entertain the fans on the field, he liked to be entertained off it too. Jim liked to party and only did such training as was necessary to get by. He only did what he had to do in order to be fit enough to produce the goods during a game. Not for him was the idea of going back in the afternoons for extra practice, the way some of his teammates did. He led the George Best lifestyle and was accorded the Best idolisation years before anybody had heard of the Irish genius. Not only did he 'do the business' for Rangers, he also did it for Scotland – especially against England, a fact that endeared him to all Scottish fans, not just Rangers ones. He played for his country on 34 occasions and, in particular, in the Scots sides that beat the Auld Enemy in 1962, 1963 and 1964, but his crowning moment was in the 3–2 win at Wembley in 1967 when he teased and tormented the English World Cup holders, making Scots everywhere feel 10ft tall.

So great was Baxter that he was accorded the honour of playing in the Rest of the World side that faced England in its Centenary match at Wembley in 1963. The following season saw Baxter at his peak, and with Rangers going well in the European Cup the signs were promising. In Vienna, however, in the second leg of their European Cup second round match, disaster struck Rangers and Baxter. With the game all but over and Gers cruising into the quarter-final, following a magnificent Baxter performance, Slim Jim was tackled by a frustrated Austrian and his leg was broken. The loss of Baxter for the quarter-final against Inter Milan was too much for Rangers, who went down 3–2 on aggregate. Every Gers fan wondered what might have been if only the great Baxter had been available to play in those two matches. By the end of March 1965 Baxter was appearing in the team again, but he would only play another eight matches for Rangers before being transferred to Sunderland at the end of that season.

A brief return to Ibrox in 1969, when Rangers were in the shadow of Jock Stein's Celtic and desperate for a saviour, fizzled out. He was no longer 'Slim Jim', and new manager Willie Waddell, believing that he was not the type of influence that he needed around, let him leave. He retired at the ridiculously young age of 30 and died in 2001, but his legend lives on – a true immortal.

Jim Baxter played 254 games and scored 24 goals. He won three League Championships, three Scottish Cups and four League Cups.

# John Greig (1961–78)

John Greig is officially Mr Rangers. A few years ago the club organised a poll to find the Greatest Ranger, and Greig was accorded that honour by the fans. He was the ultimate one-club man who played for Rangers, became its manager and worked as its PR officer after that. A quick survey of his achievements will also support his credentials. He captained club and country, earning 44 caps. He played in a record three treble-winning sides, captaining two of those. He made 857 appearances for Rangers, scoring an incredible (for a defender) 120 goals and in that time was twice voted Player of the Year by Scottish sportswriters. He won every domestic honour at least four times and captained Rangers to the European Cup-Winners' Cup trophy in 1972. On retiring as a player he was awarded the M.B.E. for his services to football.

Still, it is not just this impressive list of honours that made John Greig the 'Greatest Ranger'. It was the devotion, loyalty, hard work and leadership that he gave to the club over his lengthy career. At the time of writing, he is still working tirelessly behind the scenes on behalf of Rangers as a director. Although he joined the club in 1961, it was actually in the summer of 1962 that he truly burst on to the Ibrox scene when he replaced Jim Baxter for Rangers' ground-breaking, unbeaten tour of the Soviet Union. So great an achievement was this considered that, on its return, the team's plane was surrounded by thousands of welcoming Gers fans on the tarmac at Renfrew Airport.

Photograph © Action Images / MSI

John Greig in action for Rangers in 1975.

A statue of former Rangers captain John Greig was erected outside the Main Stand in 2001 to mark the 30th anniversary of the Ibrox disaster.

The John Greig Statue.

Jim Baxter had been on National Service at the time, and the Army refused to release him for that tour so Greig filled in and gave the side another facet with his drive, determination and tackling ability – all qualities that would complement Baxter's silky skills for the following seasons. Throughout his long career, Greig showed a versatility that would have been an asset to any team. He played in either full-back position, central defence or in midfield. During the darkest days of Celtic's nine-in-a-row years, it was Greig who was the Gers' inspiring skipper, frequently scoring a goal from long range that won his side the points. In most games, it seemed that Greig covered every blade of grass in his determination to ensure that he and his teammates did not let their fans down. For many years, fans and pundits alike agreed that Greig carried Rangers on his back – and never let them down.

Greig was a great competitor with a talent for leadership that meant no cause was lost while he was still on the field. In the brilliant team of the early 1960s he was the perfect foil for Jim Baxter, allowing him time and space to destroy the opposition because Greig would take care of any danger. Having said that, Greig's own passing ability was better than most people gave him credit for. His never-say-die spirit was in keeping with those great Gers captains of the past. At his peak, he could have left Ibrox for any number of top English clubs, but his loyalty to Rangers was never in question. That loyalty was richly rewarded in the 1970s when he captained the club to two trebles and European success.

Perhaps Greig's supreme fitness and dedication were the main factors in the longevity of his career. The greatest testimony to his resilience and consistency is the fact that he won the Football Writers' Player of the Year award twice, in 1966 and 1976. That 10-year gap had seemingly not led to any deterioration in Greig's performances. His energy, enthusiasm and fitness seemed to be no different from the younger Greig all those years before. No wonder that in 1978 65,000 fans packed into Ibrox for his testimonial match in which his Rangers team thrashed the full Scotland side bound for Argentina. It is a pity that Ally McLeod had not seen fit to include the legend in his squad as he might have had a real captain who could have driven his players on to beat Iran, a task that was beyond that sorry Scotland squad, apparently.

John Greig won five League Championships, six Scottish Cups, four League Cups and one European Cup-Winners' Cup.

# Colin Jackson (1963–82)

Colin Jackson joined Rangers straight from his Junior side Sunnybank Athletic, and most fans still think he is an Aberdonian but, in fact, he was born in London in 1946. He is one of the few Rangers who was born outside Scotland but who played for the national side. The others in this short list are John Little, Andy Goram, Richard Gough and Stuart McCall. Jackson played for Scotland on eight occasions.

Although he joined the club in 1963, it was not until the 1970–71 season that he became a regular in the first team. His patience had been tested due to the longevity and abilities of John Greig and Ronnie McKinnon in the heart of the Rangers' defence. But his long wait ended when he partnered McKinnon while Greig moved to left-back or midfield.

Jackson was a tall but slender central-defender, rather than a rugged type, but he had a tough mentality and self-belief that made him the ideal 'stopper' centre-half. Most saw him as an 'old-fashioned' centre-half in that he did his defensive duties simply and reliably, always clearing his lines first. He was well-liked and respected by the fans, who realised that he always gave 100 per cent and would never shirk a

Colin Jackson of Rangers moves in to tackle Davie Provan of Celtic.

tackle or a challenge. Jackson was certainly more mobile and quicker than most central-defenders of the day, but one of his greatest assets was his ability in the air, both in defence and attack. A career total of 40 goals from a defender who was not a penalty-taker speaks for his ability as an attacking centre-half at set pieces. He was the original 'Bomber', playing for Gers 20 years before John 'Bomber' Brown.

Two of his most memorable goals came in vital matches. In the 1979 League Cup Final against Aberdeen, with only seconds left, Jackson headed the winning goal to make it 2–1. Not for the first time he got on to the end of a perfect cross from Tommy McLean to power the ball into the net. When Gers won the title in the 1977–78 season, a win over Motherwell on the final day of the season at Ibrox was needed to clinch the Championship, and Jackson duly scored one of the goals in the 2–0 win.

He was at the height of his powers in the mid to late 1970s when he formed a rock-like partnership with Tom Forsyth at the centre of the Rangers defence, in which they complemented each other perfectly. Together they were the foundation of the Gers side that won two trebles in three seasons. Before that, Jackson's finest hour should have been the Final of the European Cup-Winners' Cup in 1972, but he was unable to play in that memorable match due to injury. An indication of how invaluable he had been to the team in that European campaign can be seen in the fact that he played in seven of the nine games and that the club awarded him a medal anyway for his services in helping get Gers to Barcelona. One of his finest displays actually came in the semi-final against Bayern Munich. Although normally a zonal defender, he was sometimes required to perform a man-marking job on occasions, especially against dangerous strikers in key games. One such opponent was the legendary goalscorer Gerd Müller, whom Jackson marked out of the game, thus nullifying the Germans' greatest threat.

Like many players of his era, Jackson enjoyed a long career thanks to the stamina and fitness built up during the Jock Wallace regime at Ibrox. Fitness and 'character' were two attributes that Wallace demanded from his players, and Jackson certainly delivered on both. At the end of the 1981–82 season, manager John Greig allowed him to leave Ibrox, but in his time as manager he never did replace this defensive stalwart.

Jackson played 505 games and scored 40 goals. He won three League Championships, three Scottish Cups and five League Cups.

# Sandy Jardine (1964–82)

How many Rangers fans know that Jardine's first name is actually William and that the 'Sandy' nickname arose from the colour of his hair? Whether or not they know this, they all will know that Jardine is a true Rangers legend. Even more remarkable for a 'modern' player is the fact that Sandy became a fans' hero while playing in the unglamorous position of right-back, rather than as a striker or as a 'flair' player. An Edinburgh lad, Jardine signed for the club in 1964, which was, unfortunately for him, just at the end of that great era when a Baxter-led Rangers dominated the domestic scene. He would know the good times and the bad with Rangers, such was his exceptional length of service with the club.

He played for Rangers from 1965 to 1982, finishing with a total of 674 games, a figure only eclipsed by his teammate John Greig and old-timer Dougie Gray. Indeed, Jardine served under five Rangers managers: Symon, White, Waddell, Wallace and Greig himself. Another tribute to Jardine's longevity is the fact that he is one of only four players to have won the Scottish Sportswriters' Player of the Year award twice but, even more remarkably, he is the only one to have achieved this with two different clubs and with the longest gap between them. Jardine won this particular award first in 1975 and then in 1986 while playing with Hearts. That year's award saw him honoured as its oldest recipient, too.

Jardine was signed by Scot Symon as a wing-half (that is a midfielder, to you younger readers) but was played in various positions by various managers before finally finding his ideal spot at right-back by Willie Waddell. Jardine had great skill, speed, stamina, determination and intelligence and eventually became a world-class full-back. So good was he that Celtic's classy Danny McGrain was required to play at left-back for the Scotland side of the mid to late 1970s. In his 38 Scotland appearances, Jardine seldom put a foot wrong.

Ironically, Jardine's Rangers debut in February 1967 came about as a result of the worst defeat in Rangers' history. At 18 years old, he was thrown in at the deep end against Hearts one week after Rangers had been knocked out of the Scottish Cup by Berwick. He did well and never looked back. By the end of that season he had even found himself up against Beckenbauer and co. as Rangers contested the 1967 European Cup-Winners' Cup Final against Bayern Munich. At the end of that match, Jardine actually swapped shirts with Der Kaiser himself. It was not to be the last time they would oppose each other in a major match.

Photograph © Action Images / MSI

Sandy Jardine in action for Rangers, December 1975.

When Davie White became Rangers manager, for a while, he experimented by playing Jardine at centre-forward, of all places. It was not as strange a decision as it might seem for Jardine could pass the ball, had an awareness of players around him and had a good shot on him. At that time, however, he was not mobile enough for that position. Still, by the end of his Ibrox career Jardine had amassed 77 goals – a great tally for a player who was essentially a defender.

Nevertheless, it was only when Willie Waddell became manager that Jardine truly flourished. It was he who switched him to right-back and whose fitness regime, supervised by Jock Wallace, increased the fitness and stamina of the players. Even more vital was the fact that Waddell sent Jardine and Willie Johnston to a specialist who coached them in sprint training. So successful was this that Jardine and Johnston eventually took part in professional sprint meetings, with Jardine actually winning a 200 metres race for a prize of £25!

The fitness gained under Jock Wallace especially, coupled with his own determination and pride, was a vital factor in the great length and quality of Jardine's career. He became, and stayed, one of the fittest players at Ibrox, no matter his age, and he played until he was 39! He is one of the few players to have twice been part of a treble-winning team.

Sandy Jardine, even in the modern game, would be considered a class act. His qualities would see him thrive into today's game as they did in the 1970s and 1980s. He was intelligent, fast, exciting, reliable, consistent and elegant. A bonus was that he was more two-footed than most players, capable of shooting with either foot. He had mobility and pace as well as stamina, allowing him to run up and down the flank all day. He was a wing-back before such a position had been created. As a defender, he could use his speed but also his brain to tackle at the opportune moment, to intercept and to nip danger in the bud. He also had the vision to cover for teammates in-field when necessary.

As a modern, attacking full-back, this vision and pace was also invaluable as Jardine was capable of creating goals as well as scoring them. For a player who was invariably joining in the Rangers' attacks, he was seldom caught out by a swift counter-attack as his vision, speed and stamina always seemed to manage to get him back into position to do the defending that was necessary.

Throughout his long service to the club, Jardine endeared himself to the fans with his ability, dedication and loyalty. He gave his all throughout the good and the not so good times at Ibrox. When manager Greig released him after the 1982 Scottish Cup Final defeat Jardine was 33, with his best days behind him. Who could have realised that he would play on with Hearts for another five years and become their assistant player-manager? He was a mainstay in that Hearts side that should have won the double in the 1985–86 season, cruelly losing out at the death in both competitions.

Despite his heroic status at Tynecastle, however, it is as a Rangers legend that Sandy Jardine will always be remembered, thoroughly deserving of his inclusion in the Ibrox Hall of Fame.

He played 674 games for Rangers and scored 77 goals. He won one European Cup-Winners' Cup, three League Championships, five Scottish Cups and five League Cups.

## Willie Johnston (1964–72 & 1980–82)

One of Rangers' great traditions seems to be that when one tremendous winger is nearing the end of his career, another small, brilliant but younger one is waiting to take over. Thus it was when Davie Wilson was superseded by the 17-year-old Willie Johnston. Although he had been signed in 1964 from a Fife Junior side, 'Bud', as he became known, was actually a Glaswegian. Making his debut for Gers at the age of 17, so spectacular were his performances that within six months he was playing for Scotland in World Cup qualifying matches, becoming the youngest international since Denis Law with whom he formed a left-wing partnership.

As a winger, Johnston was a combination of Henderson and Wilson in that he had electric pace (he was faster than either of those two) and a mesmerising dribbling ability. Also, he was more like Wilson in his goalscoring prowess. Indeed, at various points in his career he had played on the wing or as a striker through the middle with equal effect and had scored some great goals. Unfortunately, his Achilles heel was his temperament. A short fuse when fouled once too often by frustrated defenders would normally lead Bud to retaliate and end up getting himself sent off. By the end of his career he had seen the red card an astonishing 20 times – and most would have acknowledged that he was neither a hard man nor a dirty player!

As well as being brave, skilful and exciting to watch, Johnston was also a character – the type of which we see too few of nowadays in Scottish football. He was the sort

Willie Johnstone, 1981.

who could gleefully pat a defender on the head if he had just scored an own-goal or, a la Baxter, sit on the ball and tease his opponents. He was a player who gave everything and liked to play with a smile on his face, remembering that the game was there to be enjoyed. He liked to acknowledge the presence of the supporters and 'play to the gallery' whenever possible. Unfortunately, all too often his wit and back chat would get him into trouble with officialdom, with those dreaded cards being flashed once again.

This lamentable disciplinary record was the only fly in the ointment of his Ibrox career. He was thrilling to watch and a very effective member of the team, making and scoring goals from the mid-1960s onwards when, all too often, Rangers were playing second fiddle to Stein's Celtic. Indeed, not only did he score goals throughout Gers' journey to eventual success in Barcelona in the European Cup-Winners' Cup in 1972, he even scored two of the three goals in the Final. He forged a great partnership with Colin Stein, who scored the other goal in that game.

It seems that both those players were considered to be prima donnas and too individualistic for the liking of new manager Jock Wallace, and so, after the Barcelona triumph, they were transferred to different clubs in England. Johnston was transferred to West Brom after yet another suspension – this time a nine-week-long affair. There he was the same old Bud, becoming the darling of the fans, thrilling them and causing despair with his ill discipline in equal measures. His international career flourished, however, and he earned more caps while in England than he had at Ibrox. Unfortunately, after 22 caps his Scotland career ended ignominiously during the ill-fated World Cup in Argentina in 1978 when he was sent home in disgrace after a blood test found him guilty of taking a banned medication.

After his stint at West Brom, Johnston went to play in Vancouver for a while and then to Birmingham before John Greig, now Rangers manager, re-signed him for the club in 1980. As always seems to be the case, his return to the scene of former triumphs did not work out. He played a couple of seasons at Ibrox and was still capable of turning in some brilliant performances, but by now these were more infrequent than in his first spell with the club. Moreover, he had not mellowed with age. A month after his first match during this second period saw him yet again ordered off against Aberdeen. Same old Bud! He ended his career playing for Hearts at the age of 39. If his temperament had not changed then neither had his fitness, which helped him enjoy such a long and colourful career.

Willie Johnston played 393 games for the club and scored 125 goals. He won one European Cup-Winners' Cup, one Scottish Cup and two League Cups.

## Dave Smith (1966–74)

Aberdonian Dave Smith made his debut for his home-town team in 1962 at Pittodrie. By 1966, he had played 166 games and scored 13 goals for the Dons, so a number of clubs were interested in signing the silky player. Apart from Rangers, Spurs and Everton also fancied getting his signature. The Aberdeen directors would have preferred their number-one asset to go to England to avoid him playing against them and because they would have got more money for the player; however, Smith's heart was set on Ibrox so Gers got their man. In the summer of 1966 they stumped up £50,000 to secure the services of a player who became one of the first to be deployed as a 'sweeper' in the Scottish game.

What a debut season he had. The 1966–67 campaign was the season that featured Rangers' worst-ever result in the Scottish Cup when they lost to Berwick and, at the end of it, a Cup-Winners' Cup Final loss to Bayern Munich. On the road to Nuremberg Smith certainly grew up in terms of European experience. The following season, Rangers lost their chance of taking the League title away from Celtic on the last day of the season when, ironically, Aberdeen beat them at Ibrox. Unlucky, Smith left Ibrox just before Rangers did manage to regain the Championship in 1975. In his eight full seasons at Ibrox he finished second to Celtic on five occasions. He was also unlucky in terms of winning Cup medals. He appeared in the 1969 Scottish Cup Final when Celtic won 4–0 but, due to a broken leg, he missed the famous 1970 League Cup Final when Derek Johnstone scored the winner. In his Rangers career, Smith actually broke his leg twice and came back after each injury to star again. Although he picked up a medal for the Centenary Scottish Cup Final of 1973, he did not actually play in the Final after having played in every match leading up to the Hampden climax. He was unfortunate in that he played in an era when Celtic were the top dogs in the country.

Still, Smith did have some great highlights in his Rangers career, none more so that the European medal he won in 1972 in Barcelona and winning two Scotland caps in the 1960s. It was in the European campaign culminating in Barcelona that Smith was utilised by Waddell as a sweeper in the Italian style. He was the cover behind Jackson and Johnstone in some games rather than playing alongside a central-defender, which was more the norm for British sides. Scot Symon had signed Smith as an attacking midfielder, but Willie Waddell saw how best to use his defensive capabilities. He realised that Smith's positional sense, anticipation and timing were great assets when Rangers were defending. Smith was not a tough-tackling player but one who regained possession through his other qualities. Even better, he was a good passer of the ball, and with his 'educated' left foot he could use long, raking passes to start attacks quickly. It was Smith who burst forward and made the passes that resulted in Gers' first two goals against Moscow Dynamo in Barcelona. Like the man playing behind him, Willie Mathieson, Smith was very left-footed, but it was a brilliant weapon.

Fans always thought of Smith as a cool, 'classy' player – a 'silky' one. His best year was obviously 1972 and, at the end of it, he even won the Player of the Year award, ahead of such luminaries as Dalglish and the Dons' Joe Harper. In the club's centenary year, the following year, Smith played in 29 of the 34 League games as well as nine League Cup ties and every game in the Scottish Cup to the winning final against Celtic.

When Jock Wallace took over as manager, Smith found that he did not really get on with him and did not like his style of play, so it was no surprise when he moved on to Arbroath in 1974. In those days they were in the top division and were able to pay £30,000 for his transfer. The money for Gers was a bonus because Smith had more than repaid them for the £50,000 fee that the Dons had been given eight years previously.

Dave Smith played 303 games and scored 13 goals. He won one European Cup-Winners' Cup medal and one Scottish Cup medal.

# Chapter Four

# Players Elected Between 1967–69

## History of the Period

In some seasons that came during Celtic's nine-in-a-row run, a fine Rangers team would come second despite having amassed more points than in earlier seasons when the club had won the title! The 1967–68 season deserves a special mention in this respect. Celtic were the reigning European champions that season and retained their League title, but the Gers side of that campaign only lost one match (the last one against Aberdeen at Ibrox) winning 28 out of 34, scoring 93 goals and accruing a massive 61 points – yet still lost out to Celtic by two points! It was halfway through that season that the club sacked manager Scot Symon and installed Davie White, who only lasted one full season. In some seasons of this great Celtic run, Rangers would only be one or two points behind the greatest teams in Celtic's history as they continually retained their title.

Having said that, there was a prolonged stage when Rangers could not win anything. In the four seasons from 1966–67 until 1970–71 the club failed to win any of the three domestic trophies, and during this time manager Scot Symon was unceremoniously dismissed.

### MANAGER: DAVIE WHITE (1967–69)

Davie White has the unenviable distinction among Rangers managers as the Scotsman who held the position for the shortest time and as one of only two managers who failed to win a major trophy. Yet, his spell at the club had seemed to herald the dawn of a new era. In order to combat Jock Stein at Celtic, Rangers' board obviously thought that they should employ a modern, track-suit manager who spent his time out on the training pitch with the lads rather than occasionally watching from the sidelines wearing a business suit, the way Symon had done. Ironically, after the defeat in Nuremberg in the Cup-Winners' Cup Final, it had been Symon himself who had recommended the young manager to his board to be a coach at Ibrox, little realising that within five months he would have replaced him.

White had had no previous connections with the club. In the early 1960s he had been a part-time player and captain of Clyde for six years before becoming its part-time manager when John Prentice had left Clyde to become Scotland boss. He was eager to embrace modern methods and tactics and studied how other managers and clubs trained their sides and played in important matches. With this in mind, White had even been present at Celtic's European Cup Final in Lisbon and Rangers' Cup-Winners' Cup Final in Nuremberg. Initially, White was invited to take control of coaching the reserve side while Bobby Seith, a recent appointment, trained the first team. White seemed to have the right credentials to take over eventually from the traditional Symon, but nobody could have guessed just how quickly.

White's tragedy was that he was forced to take over too soon. After a few months at Ibrox, he suddenly found himself in the hot seat after Symon's sacking. On the bright side, the team was top of the League at the time, near the end of November, so he was not inheriting a side on the slide, but Seith had resigned in protest at the firing of his boss, so White was left to manage the club and coach the first team by himself. Still, the young manager had confidence in his own ability, even if others doubted that he had the necessary experience and authority to run a big club like Rangers. They also wondered if he had what it took to do battle with a wily old fox like Jock Stein to gain supremacy in Scotland.

Nevertheless, the Rangers players liked their new boss and felt comfortable with him. They seemed to appreciate his new training methods and modern outlook on the game where he was not a remote, aloof presence. Despite being perhaps more approachable than Symon, he still ensured that standards of discipline were adhered to and that they remembered that he was their boss, deserving of their respect. For the remainder of that first half-season in sole charge, his Gers side kept pace with champions Celtic and, but for dropped points in their closing run-in, might have won the title. As mentioned above, the team's only League defeat came in the final match of the season against Aberdeen at Ibrox, which meant that Celtic won the Championship by two points.

For the new season, Rangers legend Willie Thornton was appointed as White's assistant manager. It was hoped that this, with some new signings, would strengthen Gers' challenge for the title. Perhaps the best move of White's short Ibrox tenure was the signing of one player in particular – Colin Stein. This tremendous centre-forward became the fans' new hero and started scoring goals from his first appearance. Weeks later, Alex McDonald was signed to bolster the midfield and scoring capability of the side and, although he started more slowly than Stein, he too eventually became a Rangers great.

That season, however, was a case of what might have been. Dropped points again in the run-in meant that Rangers finished second to their great rivals. Due to an extremely harsh suspension, the fiery, but much sinned against, Colin Stein had missed the last seven Championship games, a fact that undoubtedly cost the side a possible title. Even worse, he missed the Old Firm Scottish Cup Final in which Rangers suffered their worst Final defeat ever. Taking the brunt of the blame was Alex Ferguson, Stein's stand-in at centre-forward, who was seen as culpable for allowing Billy McNeill to head in a first-minute goal from a corner-kick that put Rangers on the back foot from the start. The 4–0 defeat was hard for everybody at Ibrox to bear and undoubtedly did not help Davie White's standing with his board or the Rangers fans. Even a good run in the Inter-Cities Fairs Cup (now the UEFA Cup) was spoiled in the semi-final by a 2–0 aggregate defeat by eventual winners Newcastle United. The previous season had seen an identical scoreline in favour of Leeds in the quarter-final stage of that competition. The regrettable crowd trouble from the Rangers fans at St James' Park perhaps mirrored the disillusion felt by the majority of Rangers fans all over the country at that time.

In an effort to counter that feeling, at the end of the season Davie White played his last card – he re-signed Rangers' legend 'Slim Jim' Baxter. He gambled on the King of Ibrox transforming his side into winners again. Unfortunately for White, 'Slim Jim' was a shadow of his former self, at least metaphorically. Years in England, underachieving and overindulging, had seen him pile on the pounds. He was no longer the same player, and the Rangers side had changed dramatically, as had the type of football played in the Scottish League. The old adage of 'never go back' was proven true once again. The failure of Baxter to recapture his earlier glory led to the inevitability of White's sacking.

Near the end of November, Rangers faced crack Polish side Gornik in a second-round tie in the Cup-Winners' Cup. Having lost 3–1 in Poland, the tie was difficult but winnable. Despite an early Baxter goal in the first half, the Poles eventually ripped Rangers apart, winning 3–1 again after a wonderful last half hour. Rangers fans and Davie White were stunned. The next day, the Rangers board, showing the same ruthlessness that they had used on Scot Symon, dismissed White. Many were sympathetic to White, but most agreed that the job had simply been too big for him. Managerial experience, gravitas and a life imbued in Rangers' traditions were the qualities Rangers now sought, and the obvious choice stared the directors in the face – Willie Waddell. His appointment to the manager's job reunited him with his old teammate Willie Thornton, and the fans started to hope for better things again.

# Players Elected

## Alfie Conn (1968–74)

Describe a teenage prodigy who became a Rangers attacking icon in the 1970s, and most fans would immediately think of Derek Johnstone; however, the original goalscoring wonderkid at Ibrox actually pre-dated D.J. by a couple of years, and his name was Alfie Conn. Like quite a few Gers heroes before him, Conn came from a Hearts background – even more so in his case because his father was Alfie Conn, who played for the Tynecastle club in the 1950s.

Conn was a 15-year-old sensation who was much sought-after. In 1967 he actually signed for the up-and-coming Leeds team managed by Don Revie, but when he discovered that he was wanted by Rangers he knew that his destiny lay there. Revie, belying his ruthless image, rescinded the contract and Conn was allowed to join the Gers.

After less than a year at Ibrox, Conn made his debut in November 1968 in the Fairs Cup (now the UEFA Cup) against Dundalk, with Gers wining 3–0 in Ireland. He came on as a sub for the future Sir Alex Ferguson. He had just turned 16.

His Rangers career only lasted six years but he actually served under four managers: Scot Symon, Davie White, Willie Waddell and Jock Wallace. Amazingly, when he left Ibrox he was still only 22. Of course, his youthful career at Ibrox has been overshadowed by that of Derek Johnstone, but how many Gers fans realise or remember that Conn was only 18 when he, too, played in that 1970 League Cup Final when D.J. scored the winning goal, aged 16? By the time he was 20 he was helping to win the Cup-Winners' Cup in Barcelona. In that European campaign he had played in four of the nine ties and in the Final played in the centre of midfield alongside Alex McDonald. The following year, he won a Scottish Cup medal when he scored the second goal against Celtic in the 3–2 win in the centenary Cup Final. That goal typified Conn as he burst from the halfway line onto a long through ball, out-paced Billy McNeill and then slammed the ball into the net from 18 yards.

Before the emergence of Derek Johnstone, Conn had been every young Rangers fan's idol. With his long hair, broad sideburns and confident, swaggering style on the pitch, he had become an instant hero. He could shoot, he could pass the ball, had vision, was capable of the unexpected and was full of youthful energy. The young Gers fans just wanted to be like him and live the dream. And, for five years, that is exactly what Alfie did, sometimes as a striker, sometimes as an attacking midfielder. Intermittent injuries affected his form, though, and most Rangers fans reckoned that he never did fulfil his undoubted potential, although the club probably saw the best of his career.

By the time Wallace was his manager his star was on the wane. During the 1973–74 season, Conn only played in about a third of the League games and knew that the writing was on the wall. Two big English clubs were interested in him: Manchester United and Spurs. He would have preferred the glamour of United, but Tommy Docherty was their manager, and seemingly Willie Waddell did not get on with him and was reluctant to do him a favour, so it was off to London for Conn.

Rangers received £140,000 for Conn in 1974, and he became Spurs manager Bill Nicholson's last signing. Once in England, injuries and operations adversely affected his progress, and he never really made it as the star he could have been. Indicative of this was the fact that he only gained two Scotland caps. Nevertheless, he did become something of a cult figure for the Spurs fans, thanks to his style, brashness and some of those cheeky or skilful flashes that he still showed occasionally. He was the Spurs fans' equivalent of Arsenal's Charlie George.

That might have been the last we would have heard of Alfie Conn – but for Jock Stein. During the course of the 1976–77 season, the Celtic manager, anxious to regain the title from Rangers, paid Spurs £60,000 for Conn's services. He thought that Conn's flair and goalscoring prowess would enhance his side but he also probably relished the idea of upsetting Rangers by signing one of their former heroes. He succeeded. For Conn, it turned out wonderfully well on the field as that season he won his first League Championship medal and, from his point of view, even more memorably he was in the Celtic side that beat Rangers 1–0 in the Scottish Cup Final. Not many players can show two Cup winners' medals from Old Firm Finals having played for either side!

So, Alfie was Mo Johnson in reverse over a decade before Mojo. Thanks to his Celtic career, playing against Gers in a Cup Final, Conn was seen as a 'traitor' by many Gers fans, who never forgave him. Still, they should remember his youthful service to Rangers – the club he chose, after all, instead of Leeds. When Conn signed for arch-rivals Celtic, he just saw it as another job, a way to earn his living and pick up a couple of medals on the way. Who can blame him? Maybe Rangers fans should remember that he was one of those few heroes to have won a European medal for the club while scoring some memorable goals in his time at Ibrox.

Alfie Conn played 149 games and scored 39 goals. He won one European Cup-Winners' Cup, one Scottish Cup and one League Cup with Rangers.

## Colin Stein (1968–73 & 1975–77)

Until he arrived at Ibrox in 1968, Colin Stein's surname was one that had only occasioned a feeling of dread in Gers fans, being associated with the first name Jock, the Celtic manager who had become supreme in Scotland by then; however, from the start of Colin's career at Ibrox, the fans began to associate better times ahead with that particular surname. Stein's arrival would eventually mean the departure of Alex Ferguson, whose combative style of centre-forward play had been one of the brighter aspects of Rangers' performances in the previous couple of years. Stein was simply a bigger, stronger, more skilful and more prolific version of Fergie, so there was only going to be one winner in the fight for the number-nine shirt.

Hibs had accepted an offer of £90,000 from Everton, but apparently Gers manager Davie White had had 'a quiet word' with the player, and Stein had refused to move to England. After a bit of haggling, Hibs eventually accepted £100,000 in October 1968. It was the first six-figure transfer between two Scottish clubs, but if the huge fee put a burden on Stein it certainly did not show. In his initial three matches he just missed achieving consecutive hat-tricks. His debut at Arbroath saw him snatch a hat-trick, and this was followed by another at Ibrox against his old side,

Rangers' Colin Stein celebrates after scoring his goal at the European Cup-Winners' Cup Final against Moscow Dynamo, 24 May 1972. The game resulted in a 3–2 win for Rangers.

Hibs, and then in an Inter-Cities Fairs Cup tie away to Dundalk, he scored two goals. What a start! Talk about becoming an instant hero of the fans.

Still, it was not just his scoring exploits that made him a tremendous favourite of the Rangers fans, it was also his style and attitude. He was a big, strong, enthusiastic, bustling 'old-fashioned' centre-forward who rampaged through the opposing defence. Great in the air, with a good first touch and excellent ball control, he liked nothing better than taking on defenders and would seldom be found in a static position as he roamed from one flank to the other in search of the ball if the passes did not come to him. Stein's tragedy was that the club could not find him a strike partner at the time, and he seemingly had to do the work of more than one player up front.

Still, he did not complain and just got on with it, always trying his hardest for the team and showing the traditional Rangers spirit that obviously endeared him to the supporters. He was a great all-round player, and his only flaw seemed to be his suspect temperament. Too often he would be sent off for retaliation, usually after having taken too much punishment from ruthless defenders who could only stop him by foul means.

Typical of his fate was his sending off at Ibrox against Clyde in a League game near the end of the 1968–69 season. Rangers were 6–0 up with Stein playing brilliantly, already having scored a hat-trick. As he ran with the ball across the centre circle, a Clyde defender, Eddie Mulhearn, chased him forlornly and had three or four kicks at him from behind. Thanks to his short fuse, Stein could not take any more and simply stopped in his tracks, turned around and had a swipe at the Clyde man. Result? Stein sent off, while nothing happened to the instigator of the incident!

A six-week ban was the eventual outcome of the disciplinary hearing, causing Stein to miss the run-in to the League when Rangers dropped eight vital points to finish second, yet again, to Celtic. Just to rub it in, Stein also missed the Old Firm Scottish Cup Final which saw Celtic win 4–0 and marked the end of Alex Ferguson's Gers career as he was blamed for not marking Billy McNeill, who scored with a header from a corner in the very first minute. Most fans agreed that Stein would have challenged McNeill in such a situation and during the game and would have caused the Celtic defence more problems than Fergie ever could.

Colin Stein, as well as becoming a Rangers hero also became a Scotland one, eventually amassing 21 caps. In matches against the 'Auld Enemy' he invariably played well and usually managed to cause consternation among the big English defenders. In one World Cup qualifying match against Cyprus at Hampden he even managed to score four goals. Of his 97 Rangers goals, however, two still stand out as the most memorable for their sheer importance.

It was Stein who scored the opening goal of the 1972 European Cup-Winners' Cup Final in Barcelona when Rangers defeated Moscow Dynamo 3–2, and it was the same player who headed a great goal at Easter Road in 1975 to ensure that Rangers got the one point they needed to win the League title for the first time in 11 years. This was his first goal since re-signing from Coventry, the club he had been sold to after Barcelona. After another couple of seasons, during which the young Derek Johnstone had become the club's top striker, he was allowed to leave the club, but Stein left an indelible mark and, now, along with Willie Johnston from that side, he is a worthy member of Rangers' Hall of Fame.

Colin Stein played 206 games for the club and scored 97 goals. He won one European Cup-Winners' Cup and two League Cups.

The European Cup Winner's Cup won by Rangers in 1972 in Barcelona.

# Alex McDonald (1968–80)

It has become a bit of a cliché these days, but 'Doddie', as he was known, really was the fan who ended up living the dream. Like later Rangers hero Ian Durrant, he was brought up not far from Ibrox, in the Kinning Park area of Glasgow. Always a Rangers fan, he is still considered a true 'blue nose' whose popularity among the fans has never waned. In November 1968 he was signed by Davie White, who paid St Johnstone £50,000 for his services – and what value for money Rangers got.

McDonald had a relatively slow start to his Ibrox career, perhaps due to the fact that as a local boy he was desperate to do well and that his new manager did not utilise his abilities to their advantage. Once Willie Waddell became manager, however, things changed, and Doddie started to show his true worth. As a player he was energetic, passionate, tenacious, combative, fiery and incredibly fit. The Jock Wallace training regime was responsible for that fitness and, once again, the longevity of his career.

Throughout his career, McDonald showed tremendous reserves of stamina, an essential feature of his play since he seemed to cover every blade of grass, especially when surging from his own penalty area into the opposition's. Also, despite his lack of height, his grit and determination made him an ideal ball-winner in midfield. A brilliant sense of timing was also invaluable as it enabled him to make runs into the opposition box and often finish the move off with a goal.

Surprisingly, for a small man he was a great header of the ball and, despite his reputation as being a bit of a terrier, he had a fine touch with the passing ability to bring others into the game. It is probably safe to say, though, that his biggest asset was his knack of scoring important goals in the big games. These generally came about due to his ability to make perfectly-timed runs into the opposition penalty box, almost sneaking past defenders to get on to the end of an expert chip from players like Tommy McLean. McDonald's 'blind side' running resulted in many a vital goal. Maybe his lack of size helped him to lose markers, although you would have thought that after years of watching his trademark runs, opposition managers and players would have been on the alert for them. Apparently not!

McDonald's industry and determination were qualities that Waddell wanted all his Rangers players to show in matches, but he wanted his players

Photograph © Action Images / MSI

Alex McDonald (left) and Sandy Jardine (right), 1 May 1972.

to be disciplined too. Unfortunately, McDonald's greatest weakness was his fiery temperament, which resulted in him being sent off on more than one occasion. Waddell tried to channel McDonald's aggression which, for a midfielder, was an attribute as long as it could be controlled. On the whole, it was. After a sending off against Celtic it was five years before his next one.

McDonald's first major honour was taking part in the 1970 League Cup Final against Celtic, a match won by a header from 16-year-old Derek Johnstone. Doddie was not to know then that five years later he would score the winning goal against Celtic in the Final of that same competition. As memorable as those Cup wins were, neither could compete with his experience of being part of the Gers side that won the European Cup-Winners' Cup in Barcelona in 1972. After that European victory, he was an integral part of the side that would win two trebles in three seasons a few years later.

McDonald, throughout his Rangers career, managed to score goals in the Finals of Scottish Cups and League Cups, but he could also do this on the European stage, scoring against great sides of the calibre of Juventus and Ajax. Even top-class defenders were obviously caught out by his tremendous runs into the box. This expertise could have been used more often in the international arena. He should certainly have gained more than his solitary cap, even though the Scots side of the 1970s was littered with brilliant midfield players.

In 1980, for a fee of £30,000, McDonald left Ibrox to become the player-manager of Hearts, and he was followed soon afterwards by Sandy Jardine as his assistant. Their management skills almost brought off the double for the Tynecastle side. Later, McDonald became one of the best managers that Airdrie ever had, taking the club to two Scottish Cup Finals, only losing out to Rangers and Celtic respectively – no mean feat. His management style had been in keeping with his playing one. He had been energetic, enthusiastic, committed, determined and combative – all those qualities that would see him enter the Rangers' Hall of Fame in due course.

Alex McDonald played 503 games for Rangers scoring 94 goals. He won one European Cup-Winners' Cup, three League Championships, four Scottish Cups and four League Cups.

# Chapter Five

# Players Elected Between 1969–72

## History of the Period

Adding to the gloom of being second best to Celtic was the second Ibrox Disaster in January 1971, when 66 Rangers fans died on stairway 13 near the end of the Old Firm Ne'er Day game. This terrible tragedy, however, was the motivation for the building of the present-day stadium, which is one of the few in the top category of UEFA stadia with its five-star rating.

Making up for those dark days when Celtic dominated were such triumphs as the League Cup Final win against Celtic in 1970, thanks to the 16-year-old Derek Johnstone, and, of course, the winning, in Barcelona, of the European Cup-Winners' Cup in 1972.

The beginning of the 1970s saw another manager, Davie White, sacked and a new manager installed in the shape of playing legend Willie Waddell, who tried to revitalise the whole club by going back to traditional values but using modern methods.

### MANAGER: WILLIE WADDELL (1969–1972)

Waddell had been one of Rangers' greatest wingers when bursting down the right during the 1930s, 1940s and early 1950s. The determination, grit, skill and love of Rangers that he had shown throughout his career was therefore called upon as the club looked for a saviour. At the time of his appointment, he was working as a football journalist for the *Daily Express* but, prior to that, he had been the most successful manager in the history of Kilmarnock for eight years, climaxing with a

League Championship win in 1964–65. Most observers saw him as perhaps the only man who could challenge the supremacy of Jock Stein in the Scottish game.

Waddell saw his immediate job as one of restoring the image of the club, instilling pride into his players and, once again, making Rangers the most respected club in the country. He promised his staff that he would be hard-working, dedicated and always put the needs of the club first – and he expected his players to do the same. He would be hard, disciplined but fair. Rangers' traditions would be re-invoked, and first-team places would go to players on merit. Youngsters who proved themselves in terms of ability and industry would be rewarded by a first-team place. Although Waddell was seen as similar to Jock Stein, he was more like Scot Symon in terms of reverence for tradition, even if he did understand and utilise more modern methods and tactics.

As the season progressed, Waddell decided which players he could use, which he could rely on and which were past their sell-by date. He also concluded that his players were not fit enough and instigated double training sessions, which also might have helped him weed out the weak or the unwilling in his quest for success. Among the first of the old guard to go in favour of youth were the likes of Baxter, Davie Provan and Orjan Persson. Others would be played in a different position and become much more successful. The likes of Sandy Jardine would be converted to right-back, becoming one of the best in the world in that position. Jardine along with Willie Johnston would be given specialist sprint training in order to increase their speed.

The strength of Waddell's personality was usually enough to get things done and get the players training and playing as hard as he desired. Near the end of the season, many of the backroom staff were allowed to leave in order that Waddell could bring in his own appointees. Among them, significantly, was Hearts' assistant manager Jock Wallace, who became the first-team coach. The following season it was Wallace who took the training sessions, allowing Waddell to be slightly more removed from his players than Davie White had been. They still realised who was boss, however, and his team talks and presence at training sessions made them understand who it was they each had to impress.

The initial months of the Waddell reign were seen as a honeymoon period in which the new manager had the time to ascertain the strengths and weaknesses of the club before formulation of his plan of action, but Waddell knew that results would have to improve from the following season onwards. Jock Wallace's tough training regime was started with the now infamous Gullane sand dunes becoming a focal point of the players' stamina training – and dread. Indeed, it was Wallace who increasingly took care of the players' conditioning while leaving Waddell to do all the other duties that were part of his remit. They became a new kind of management partnership. Like Struth, Waddell always sought to maintain standards and ensure that the Rangers players had the best of everything when it came to travelling or eating on trips abroad. In return, the players were expected to show the kind of behaviour that upheld the reputation of the club. Woe betide any player who let down the club in any way!

Waddell's need to win a major trophy of some kind was satisfied in his first full season in charge. Based on his own experience as a 15-year-old debutant for Rangers, Waddell always believed that if you were good enough, you were old enough. This philosophy led to him giving youth a chance where possible and culminated in his first Rangers success. It was in October 1970 that a 16-year-old Derek Johnstone headed the winning goal in the League Cup Final against Celtic, justifying Waddell's faith in the youngster. Unfortunately, that would be Waddell's only success that season. Once again, Rangers suffered from inconsistency, leaving them in fourth place in the table, but they fared better in Cup competitions and reached the Final of the Scottish Cup. It was no fairytale end to the season, however, as Celtic got revenge for their League Cup defeat by winning 2–1 in a replay after Derek Johnstone had again scored in the 1–1 draw previously. Despite losing, Rangers' disappointment was reduced by the fact that they qualified for the following season's European Cup-Winners' Cup, a tournament that they actually went on to win.

That European campaign turned out to be the highlight of Waddell's second and final season in charge at Ibrox. Victory in Barcelona more than made up for the absence of success in any of the domestic competitions. Perhaps that success had eluded the team because it had focussed so intently on Europe throughout the season. Or, maybe once again, it was just the dreaded inconsistency that every side fears. On their day, Rangers could seemingly beat any team, as victory over the mighty Bayern Munich had proved, but they still could not overtake Celtic in the marathon that was the League race.

Apart from European triumph, Waddell's most telling role while manager came in the wake of the Ibrox Disaster that happened in January 1971 when 66 fans lost

Glasgow Rangers Football Club General Manager Willie Waddell speaks to the media on 3 January 1971. Sixty-six Rangers football fans died after a match between Celtic and Rangers at Ibrox Park. Initial reports suggested the tragedy had been caused by supporters rushing back up the stairs, after a late Rangers goal, colliding with people leaving the stadium. But a public inquiry discounted this theory and said the deaths were the result of the crush of fans pouring down stairway 13. The disaster remains the worst in the history of Scottish football.

their lives. Waddell's dignity, concern and organisational skills all played a big part in steering the club through a most difficult time. He took the weight of responsibility dealing with the media and legal enquiries while ensuring that there was club representation at each victim's funeral or visits to the injured in hospital. It was fortunate that, in its hour of need, Rangers had a great club servant who commanded the public's total respect.

At the end of the following season, after the historic victory in Barcelona, Waddell became the general manager of the club, allowing Wallace to take his place as team manager. The Ibrox Disaster, however, had motivated Waddell to rebuild the stadium and gradually, thanks to the profit-making phenomenon of Rangers Pools, he would oversee the transformation of Ibrox into one of the world's safest and most modern stadia. Like all of his predecessors, his dictum was that only the best was good enough for Rangers and its fans. The new Ibrox was his tribute to the victims of The Disaster.

Waddell, by then, had become managing director of the club and then, eventually, a director. In its long and illustrious history, Rangers had seldom had a more loyal and effective servant over such a span of decades.

As manager, Willie Waddell won one European Cup-Winners' Cup and one League Cup.

# *Players Elected*

## Derek Johnstone (1970–83 & 1985–86)

For such a versatile player, it is really amazing that Johnstone still ended up one of Rangers' highest-ever goalscorers – despite the fact that for quite a chunk of his career he played at centre-half, not to mention the occasional spell in midfield. He must be one of the few Rangers who played in each area of the field except goalkeeper. Even more surprising is that he also did this for Scotland. Nevertheless, despite spending a lot of his time away from the front line, Johnstone was Rangers' top post-war League scorer until that man Ally McCoist overtook him in the late 1980s.

It has become a cliché in football to talk about certain players having a storybook career, being a real-life Roy of the Rovers, but the aforementioned Super Ally was one of those. However, Derek Johnstone had already acted out a similar script in the 1970s.

Derek Johnston, 1975.

The most memorable feature of Derek Johnstone's game was his heading ability. It was this that won many a match for Rangers, especially important games. So, it was appropriate that it was this skill that brought him to the attention of the general football public at the tender age of 16. The start of his Ibrox career was truly fairytale stuff. Although he had made his Rangers debut at Ibrox against Cowdenbeath in a 5–0 win, scoring twice, his real fame started a month later when Willie Waddell and Jock Wallace decided to throw this skinny kid in at the deep end in the League Cup Final of 1970 against Celtic at Hampden.

It could have been an ordeal for any youngster. Rangers were up against a Celtic side that would win the title for the sixth time in a row that season. They had already won the League Cup for five consecutive seasons and, to make the whole attempt at stopping Celtic much harder, Gers' inspirational skipper John Greig missed the match due to flu. Johnstone had only been told that he would be playing the day before the game and was advised to get a good night's sleep. Whether or not in his dreams he scored the winner the next day is irrelevant, because that is exactly what he did in reality.

It is a truism that there is no better way for a newcomer to get the Rangers fans on his side than to score a winning goal against Celtic. So, from the moment Johnstone's golden head nodded in the winner, 'D.J.' became an instant hero. Although still a boy, he was 6ft tall, with power and determination, not to mention his great ability to leap. He could also shoot with both feet. For a big lad he was mobile without being fast and was good at linking with his fellow forwards and midfield men. When playing at the back he was obviously great in the air, but he could also read a game and anticipate danger. His tackling was efficient, and as a ball-playing centre-half he was useful at starting counter-attacks. He was simply a great all-rounder.

In his debut season, Johnstone scored six goals from 13 starts, but that was just the beginning of an avalanche of Rangers goals. Still, even this early in his career, he was showing his versatility. For instance, in the European Cup-Winners' Cup run to Barcelona, Johnstone played as a striker in the quarter- and semi-finals but in the Final itself played at centre-half in place of the injured Colin Jackson. It was this ability that led to sportswriters calling him 'the new John Charles' – a reference to the giant Welshman from the 1950s who played for Juventus and Wales in both positions with distinction.

Although he became one of the top players of the 1970s, Johnstone was only accorded a mere 14 caps, a disgraceful tally for such a prodigious talent. One reason might have been the consistency of the likes of Dalglish and Jordan ahead of him in the international queue. Another possible reason could have been that he preferred to play in central defence and switched between this and up front. At the end of the 1977–78 season, he had scored 38 goals and was the leading domestic scorer in the squad that went to the World Cup in Argentina, and yet he still could not get into the side when the team was struggling. Maybe Ally McLeod would have kept his job if he had given Johnstone a try instead of his favourite, Joe Harper.

If Johnstone had spent his entire career up front, who knows how many goals he would have scored by the end of it? This is especially intriguing when we remember that he had strike partners who ranged from Colin Stein and Derek Parlane to Gordon Smith and that he could have benefited from crosses by Tommy McLean and Davie Cooper.

In his early days at Ibrox, Cup wins were the only honours that Johnstone would gain, but once Jock Wallace had turned Rangers around the League title was another honour to be added to D.J.'s list. His career was littered with Cup-winning goals but also title-clinching ones. For instance, when Rangers won the title at Tannadice in 1976, Johnstone headed the winning goal after precisely 22 seconds. His manager actually missed it as he had not taken his seat in the dug-out at that point! In the Cup Final of that treble-winning season, D.J. headed the first goal against Hearts in 45 seconds. At least Wallace managed to see that one!

Unfortunately, after the second treble-winning season of 1977–78, Johnstone never seemed to be totally happy at Ibrox. At the start of the next season he handed in a transfer request to new manager, John Greig. He was persuaded to withdraw his request and was made the club captain as well as being allowed to play in central defence from then on. Naturally, thereafter his scoring became less prolific and the player never seemed to be completely happy in this new Gers side. In 1983, he was transferred to Chelsea for £30,000.

Once Jock Wallace became manager for the second time, however, he re-signed a heftier Johnstone, but this move was not a success as the player's best days were behind him, and he found himself playing in a struggling team. With the arrival of Graeme Souness in 1986 as manager, he was given a free transfer, a rather sad end to a glittering Rangers career.

Derek Johnstone played 546 games for Rangers, scoring 210 goals. He won one European Cup-Winners' Cup, three League Championships, five Scottish Cups and five League Cups.

## Peter McCloy (1970–86)

Peter McCloy is a goalkeeper who tends to be under-rated, even by many of the Rangers fans who saw him play, but the fact that he spent 16 years at Ibrox, mostly as the first-team 'keeper, and that he is only one of seven 'keepers in the Hall of Fame that covers the 136 years of the club's history, surely testifies to his quality.

Nicknamed 'The Gas Meter' or more commonly 'The Girvan Lighthouse', McCloy was a towering 'keeper. The latter nickname was a reference to his birthplace in 1946 and his height of 6ft 4in. He might have been the tallest Gers 'keeper of all time. Ironically, he was an out-field player until the age of 15 when he started playing in goal for his youth team. He was spotted by Motherwell scouts, given a couple of trials and signed for them at the tender age of 17. When he was 18 he made the biggest decision of his young life when he chose to play football rather than become assistant pro golfer at Turnberry.

He played for 'Well until December 1969 when Waddell signed him in a swap deal for Herron and Watson, even though at that point he was in the reserves. Waddell obviously saw something in the player that he believed could be developed, and so he arrived at Ibrox as the new manager's first major signing. McCloy would play under four Rangers managers: Waddell, Wallace (twice) Greig and Souness; although, by this time, McCloy was in the reserves mainly, and one of Souness' first moves was to buy English international Chris Woods to replace the first-choice Walker and veteran McCloy.

During Jock Wallace's regime, McCloy was as fit as the Alex McDonalds of the time because he did exactly the same training as the rest of the squad and got very little specialised 'keeper training, despite the fact that Wallace himself had been a goalkeeper. Indeed, McCloy was one of the best runners at the club.

Like many Rangers 'keepers before him, McCloy soon discovered that the hardest part of goalkeeping at Ibrox was the concentration factor. Since Gers dominated most games, it was easy for a 'keeper to lose his focus when he might only be called on to make one save in the entire 90 minutes, even with the match already won. A high-profile 'keeper like a Rangers goalkeeper would always be slaughtered in the

Photograph © Action Images / Sporting Pictures / Nick Kidd

Ally McCoist and Peter McCloy celebrate with the trophy won at the 1984 Skol Cup Final against Celtic at Hampden Park on 25 March 1984.

press (and by the fans) if a careless goal was lost and could be attributed to poor goalkeeping. Most older Rangers fans can remember the sight of McCloy dangling from the crossbar in the 1978 Scottish Cup Final against Aberdeen, thinking that a mis-hit shot had gone over when it was actually resting in the net.

Unfortunately, some Rangers fans remember such errors McCloy made and too often forget the brilliant saves that allowed the rest of the side to push on and win vital matches, especially in Europe. It was probably in European competition that McCloy had his best games – maybe due to the fact that, especially in away games, Gers were mainly under the cosh and had to withstand more pressure than in a dozen games in domestic football. With his great experience of European football he really should have won more caps than the four he did.

One of McCloy's most memorable features was his ability to kick the ball, especially from his hand. His prodigious kicks became the stuff of legend. When Peter kicked the ball from the edge of his penalty area it was like a shell being fired from a howitzer, causing havoc when it landed among the enemy. These kicks could become a valuable weapon in Gers' attacking armoury of the 1970s. Such a kick created Rangers' third goal for Willie Johnston in the Cup-Winners' Cup victory in 1972. In 1976, in a Scottish Cup semi-final, it rescued Gers who were 2–1 down to 'Well when McCloy's kick into the opposition area allowed Derek Johnstone to head past the 'keeper as the ball bounced up. Even by 1984 McCloy's kicks were still effective, as in Gers' 3–2 League Cup Final win he launched a 50ft-high 'special' that bounced into the Celtic area for Sandy Clark to head sideways for McCoist to net. There were many more such occasions.

Of many great European performances, a few brilliant ones stand out: in away matches against Cologne in the European Cup of 1978–79, Valencia in the Cup-Winners' Cup, defying such superstars as Bonhof and Kempes, and in Munich on the way to that Barcelona final.

In his time at Ibrox, McCloy had had to see off rivals such as Stewart Kennedy and Jim Stewart for the number-one jersey, and despite replacing the big 'keeper temporarily nobody ever really took over as custodian until Jock Wallace's final season when Nicky Walker made the position his own, by which time, of course, McCloy had been at Ibrox for 16 years. He can be proud of his service to the club and the various managers he served under. He deserves to be the only Gers 'keeper to have won a European medal for the club.

He played 644 games and had 257 shut-outs. He won one European Cup-Winners' Cup, one League Championship, four Scottish Cups and four League Cups.

## Tommy McLean (1971–82)

Tommy McLean was one of the most skilful players ever to wear a Rangers shirt. He became a Gers winger, but not one who followed in the Ibrox tradition of his predecessors. His style of play straddled two eras and two roles: one, the out-and-out winger, the other the modern, right-sided midfield player. Like the legends before him such as Waddell, Henderson and Scott, McLean was capable of dancing down the wing, but he had such an intelligent, perceptive footballing brain that he could never really be classed as a 'traditional' Scots winger – apart from the fact that he was only 5ft 4in tall. He may not have had the power of Waddell, the pace of Scott or the trickery of Henderson but his ability, awareness and skill made him capable of being just as effective as a creator of goals as any of those greats in whose footsteps he followed.

Like most brilliant wingers, McLean had excellent ball control but, unusually for a winger, he could pass and cross the ball with either foot. His trademark precise passes and crosses created numerous chances for his strikers. He was renowned for the accuracy of his passing, and this had only come about by constant practice when he was a youngster. Goalscorers such as Derek Parlane, Derek Johnstone, Gordon Smith and Alex McDonald were the beneficiaries of McLean's resulting expertise.

Willie Waddell signed McLean from Kilmarnock in 1971, and he knew exactly what he was getting. After all, it was Waddell who had signed him previously when he had been the Killie manager! Already a Scottish international and League Championship winner while at Kilmarnock, in McLean Rangers were getting the finished article. The fee of £65,000 was enough to convince Killie to let him go, but Rangers got a player who was worth so much more to them.

Like quite a few players, it took McLean a few months to settle at Ibrox and adjust to his new surroundings and methods in training. Coming in at under 10st, the weight training did not do him any favours and he lost some of his sharpness. A chat with Jock Wallace saw his training regime altered to suit his physique and soon the real Tommy McLean was terrorising the opposition defenders once again. Another difficulty was the fact that he was seen by the fans to be taking over from

Tommy McLean in action for Rangers, December 1975.

their favourite, Willie Henderson, so he had to win them over with his totally different style of play which involved passing the ball more often than dribbling with it.

Nevertheless, the fans eventually accepted McLean as a different kind of winger but no less valuable for all that. Taking part in the Cup-Winners' Cup Final in Barcelona and contributing brilliantly in the previous rounds of the tournament ensured that McLean was appreciated by the supporters. They could see that in European football McLean's quick breaks were priceless when dealing with ultra-defensive sides such as Torino. Not only could McLean get to the byline or near it, but his crosses were usually accurate and telling. Although he must have made hundreds of goals for his Rangers teammates through his vision and accuracy, he also managed to score 57 himself, which is a respectable total for a player who was essentially a creative midfielder or winger.

McLean retired in 1982 and became assistant manager to John Greig before becoming a manager in his own right with such clubs as Morton, Motherwell, Hearts and Dundee United. Then for a spell he was a coach to the youngsters at Murray Park. He certainly had a lot of expertise to pass on to younger players.

Tommy McLean played 452 games for Rangers and scored 57 goals. He won one European Cup-Winners' Cup, three League Championships, four Scottish Cups and three League Cups.

# Chapter Six

# Players Elected Between 1972–78

## History of the Period

The mid-to-late 1970s, a period which saw the end of Jock Stein's dominance, became a happier time for Rangers with the winning of the Championship in 1974 after a 10-year gap and two trebles in the following three seasons under Jock Wallace, who had been promoted from coach under Waddell.

In the European Cup-Winners' Cup Rangers defeated Moscow Dynamo in Barcelona, winning in its third appearance. Surely, no club could have deserved to lift the trophy more than Rangers. A 3–2 defeat of their old foes Moscow Dynamo seemed a fitting end to a brilliant campaign. On the way to that Final, Rangers had had to knock out the Cup winners of some of the Continent's most formidable footballing countries. First Rennes of France were eliminated before it was the turn of Sporting Lisbon of Portugal. Then, Italians Torino fell, before revenge was gained over the mighty Bayern Munich in the semi-final. At last Rangers had won a European trophy, and the hard way at that!

### MANAGER: JOCK WALLACE (1972–78 & 1983–86)

Like Bill Struth all those years before him, by the time Wallace became the club's manager he was already well versed in the traditions of Ibrox and well-known to the players whose boss he suddenly had become. As the hands-on coach, Wallace had obviously gained the respect of the Rangers players already, so moving up to the manager's office was not such a dramatic transformation, especially as Willie Waddell was still around and now as general manager – in effect, he was Wallace's boss.

Photograph © Action Images / MSI

Manager Jock Wallace talking to the players before the Scottish Cup Final in 1973. Rangers triumphed with a 3–2 win over Celtic.

Although born and brought up in Midlothian, Wallace had been a Rangers supporter from his youth, so becoming the manager at Ibrox was the proverbial dream come true. A goalkeeper, he spent most of his career playing in the lower Leagues in England and Scotland, but this was no handicap. He probably remembered that the greatest Rangers manager, Bill Struth, had been an athlete rather than a football player. Wallace eventually became the player-manager of little Berwick Rangers, just in time to knock their illustrious namesakes out of the Scottish Cup in the club's biggest upset until then. This success undoubtedly hastened his departure and, a year later, he went to Hearts as assistant manager.

A former soldier, Wallace was a strict disciplinarian and believed that supreme fitness was the basic requirement of any football player. Stamina and endurance were prerequisites for any Wallace player, and his training regimes set out to produce such men. When Willie Waddell became Rangers' manager and came to the conclusion that the players were nowhere near fit enough, it was the logical step to bring in Jock Wallace to rectify the situation. Fitness, aligned with spirit and character, was the first step on the path to rejuvenating the Ibrox club. Wallace was proud of his own fitness and would never ask his charges to do what he could not do himself, a fact that created even more respect for him among the players.

After becoming manager, Wallace showed his ruthless and single-minded nature by moving on two of the fans' heroes of Barcelona: Colin Stein and Willie Johnston. Wallace had decided that they were a bad influence, too individualistic, too 'big for their boots' and could not benefit the team in the long run, so he had them transferred. Gradually, he built up his own pool of players to create a side that would challenge Jock Stein's Celtic. In fact, his first success came in the Centenary Scottish Cup Final against Celtic when the famous Tom Forsyth 'screamer' from 6in won the Cup with a 3–2 victory in 1973 – Wallace's first season in the hot seat.

It would be two seasons later, however, before Wallace managed to achieve what every Rangers manager was expected to – the League Championship. So dominant had been the Celtic sides, winning nine titles in a row, that the format of the League was changed after the 1974–75 season. Thus, this was the last season of the old First Division before the advent of the new Premier League, designed to encourage fiercer competition. The irony was that Wallace's Rangers stopped Stein's run of consecutive titles without the aid of a new format. Further irony came from the fact that the once discarded and now re-signed Colin Stein scored the goal at Easter Road in the 1–1 draw that brought the Championship back to Ibrox for the first time in 10 years. Wallace had shaped a squad of players in his own image that could succeed where so many in the recent past had failed.

The following season, Rangers created yet another 'first' as they became the first club to win the new Premier League. Not only that, but it also became a treble-winning season. A blank season in the following campaign could be explained by the dreaded injury curse to key players such as Tom Forsyth, before Wallace repeated his treble feat in 1977–78 after adding three skilful players to his team that had won the treble in 1975–76: Russell, Smith and Cooper. The fact that two trebles in three seasons had only ever been achieved once before – by a Jock Stein Celtic side – puts Wallace's success into perspective. 'The Big Man' was at the height of his powers whereas Jock Stein was basically sacked as the Celtic manager, having been replaced by Billy McNeill.

Then, amazingly, Jock Wallace gave it all up. He suddenly resigned as manager and his captain John Greig was catapulted into the manager's office. The next season saw former playing rivals and Old Firm captains, Greig and McNeill, battle it out as managers of their clubs!

Wallace's resignation was accepted by the Rangers board 'with regret'. To his eternal credit, Wallace never did reveal the reasons for his abrupt departure. He loved Rangers too much to cause further controversy and unrest. Rumours abounded, such as he was annoyed at the lack of funds allocated to buy new players, or that he felt that his true worth had not been recognised by the club either in terms of his salary or status within the club, or that his relationship with Willie Waddell had deteriorated. Whatever the truth, it was never confirmed by Jock Wallace, who eventually became the manager of Leicester, after a spell in Seville, of all places, despite the fact that Rangers were always his only love.

That love and respect was eventually returned in 1983 following the resignation of John Greig. With the club in disarray, following the rejection of the manager's job by luminaries Alex Ferguson and Jim McLean, Rangers needed a sure hand on the rudder, and the character of Jock Wallace was the means by which the Rangers board hoped to change the club's ailing fortunes. As with players, the old saying 'never go back' was eventually proved true of managers.

When Wallace took over from Greig early in the 1983–84 season, Rangers were already well adrift in sixth place in the League race. This, along with the poor squad of players he had inherited, meant that Wallace knew that the League was gone already. His first task was to restore morale and pride in the players and move on the following season. He let the players know that the opportunity was there for any player to stake a first-team claim, and he also bought in a few such as Bobby Williamson and Nicky Walker. Still, he did manage to win the League Cup in his first season, beating Celtic 3–2 in the Final, and he repeated this feat the next season when Dundee Utd were beaten 1–0.

In the League, however, nothing really changed. The quality and depth of squad was not there, and inconsistency saw Rangers fall to fourth and then fifth place by the end of Wallace's second full season in charge. It was inevitable that the board would sack him. That came as no surprise. The shock, though, was that Rangers appointed its first-ever player-manager – and that man was Graeme Souness.

Jock Wallace won three League Championships, three Scottish Cups and four League Cups.

# *Players Elected*

## Tom Forsyth (1972–82)

Fans of all clubs have always had a special place in their hearts for the sort of player who used to be known as the 'iron man' of the team. This usually meant that he was the type of player who would be hard, ferocious, the kind who would tackle a rhino – and win, thanks to his strength, determination and fearlessness. He was also usually the guy who wore his heart on his sleeve and genuinely seemed to play for the jersey, rather than merely kiss it. Tom Forsyth was such a player.

The Rangers fans who adored his style christened him 'Jaws' – a nickname he detested – in homage to the film that had been the blockbuster of the 1970s and the fact that his tackles could bite your legs; however, this nickname did not reflect at all the ability of the man. He was always a fair, honest player with more skill than he was given credit for, especially in his passing. After all, he had started out a midfield player at Motherwell before being converted to a central-defender at Ibrox by Jock Wallace.

A Glaswegian, Forsyth was delighted to sign for Rangers in October 1972 for a fee of £40,000. He already had one Scotland cap, and his move to Rangers helped him garner many more. Jock Wallace obviously believed that Forsyth was the player who could best complement Colin Jackson in central defence, and how it worked! His strength in the tackle, mobility and reading of the game made him the ideal foil for Jackson. In his first season, it was ironic that his most memorable moment came from scoring a goal. This happened in the Centenary Scottish Cup Final of 1973 when he scored the winning goal from all of 6in to give Gers a 3–2 victory over Celtic. He had certainly been a talisman for the club as he had not played in a losing Gers side since his arrival, so he was not going to let an Old Firm Cup Final spoil his record. Every Gers fan who saw it will remember his goal forever as the ball had bounced off one post then the other before Forsyth scraped it over the line with his studs before running away deliriously in celebration.

It was a dream start to Forsyth's Rangers career, but in the following years he was also part of the team that brought the League title back to Ibrox in 1975, after an 11-year gap, before winning two trebles in three seasons in 1975–76 and 1977–78. Forsyth's contribution in the winning of those trebles cannot be underestimated. His defensive expertise allied to a determination, strength and will to win combined

Tom Forsyth.

to make him a formidable barrier to opposing forwards. It is significant that the barren season in-between those trebles saw Forsyth miss almost a third of the League games played due to various injuries.

If Forsyth is remembered by Gers fans for his '73 Cup Final goal, then he is best remembered by Scotland fans for one particular tackle. This happened at Hampden in 1976 when Scotland played England. With Scotland winning 2–1 and with only a minute to go, ace English striker Mick Channon was put through by a great pass threaded through the defence. Channon was bearing down on goal, just inside the penalty area, with only the 'keeper to beat, when Forsyth caught up with him. Thankfully, Forsyth was the master of the legal sliding tackle and his challenge, from behind, resulted in the ball being swept away to safety just as Channon was about to pull the trigger. Perfect timing and technique had saved the day. An error on Forsyth's part would have resulted in either a goal or a penalty.

If that had been his finest moment in a Scotland game, then the pinnacle of his international career must have been when he captained his country against Switzerland, also in 1976. He eventually amassed 22 caps, and he was also unfortunate enough to be part of the squad that failed so miserably in the 1978 World Cup in Argentina. Unlike some of the others, however, nobody could ever have accused Tom Forsyth of not giving his all for the cause.

By the early 1980s Forsyth's best days were behind him as he picked up niggling injuries more and more frequently. In March 1982, he had to retire due to injury and eventually joined former teammate Tommy McLean as his assistant manager at Morton before the pair managed Motherwell and then Hearts. As one of Gers' greatest defenders and a fans' icon, he is rightly installed in Rangers' Hall of Fame.

Tom Forsyth played 326 games and scored six goals. He won three League Championships, four Scottish Cups and two League Cups.

## Davie Cooper (1977–89)

Apart from that of Jim Baxter, Davie Cooper must have had the most effective left foot ever used by a Rangers player. It was the cause of so much torment to opposition players through the years and the recipient of such adulation from the Rangers fans that when his testimonial match against Bordeaux was played on a Friday night, inside Ibrox was a sell-out crowd with 5,000 fans locked outside the gates. Years later Cooper was elected to the Hall of Fame and included in the composite Gers side that was considered Rangers' greatest ever.

Incredibly, and tragically, less than seven years after that Testimonial, Davie Cooper was dead. On 23 March 1995, a short while after his 39th birthday, he died of a brain haemorrhage in Glasgow's Southern General Hospital, just a mile or so away from Ibrox Stadium. The day before, at Clyde's Broadwood Stadium, he had been coaching youngsters along with former Celt, Charlie Nicholas, when he had become ill and been taken to hospital. His sudden death devastated football fans everywhere.

It was Jock Wallace who had signed the magical winger in the summer of 1977 from Clydebank for £100,000, and what a bargain that was! He was not only buying a brilliant left-winger but a Rangers fan to boot. If you examine Cooper's time at Ibrox, however, it could be claimed that, as well as being one of Gers' greatest players, he was also one of its unluckiest. He started as a Rangers player in a great side that would go on to win the treble that season and, by the end of his time at Ibrox, he would be playing in another brilliant Rangers team that dominated under the management of Graeme Souness, filled with players such as McCoist, Butcher, Gough and Wilkins. Unfortunately, in between, for too much of his time, Cooper played in a succession of mediocre Gers sides struggling through the worst spell in the club's history.

Arguably, Cooper's first season was his best. He played in every competitive Rangers match, bar one – a League game in March. Thus, he played in 54 games and won each of the domestic honours at the first time of asking. He was no doubt helped by the fact that he had taken an instant liking to Jock Wallace and realised that his manager had confidence in his ability and trusted him to perform. Wallace gave Cooper the freedom to do his own thing, and how it paid off!

It quickly became obvious that although Cooper was an individual talent, a genius on the ball, he fitted in perfectly with the overall team pattern. He struck up a great understanding with midfield man Bobby Russell and complemented the play of Tommy McLean on the opposite flank. Although he did not possess the dangerous pace of some wingers, Cooper's skill made him more than capable of getting away from defenders. He had tremendous ball control and a great first touch that gave him time to size up the situation before making his moves. He

Davie Cooper, 1985.

Photograph © Action Images / Sporting Pictures

twisted, turned and could change direction before seemingly gliding past players as if they had been mesmerised – just like the fans.

Furthermore, all this was done with that magical left foot that was capable of blistering drives that threatened to rip the net apart at times, whether from open play or free-kicks just outside the area. It could also be used to send others through with sublime passes, reminiscent of those made by Baxter over two decades previously. Especially effective was Cooper's reverse pass that was normally clever and disguised enough to open up the best of defences. All these qualities were used to the full in that initial season when the treble was won thanks to Cooper's ability being utilised by the running power of Smith and McDonald, coupled with the passing skills of McLean and Russell and the predatory instincts of Derek Johnstone.

Unfortunately, after that great season, it has to be admitted that over the next five years Cooper was an under-used and underachieving genius. In the sterility of the early 1980s, Cooper all but carried the Rangers teams. In the big games, the fans recognised that Cooper was the one man the opposition feared and that he was the brightest hope for achieving a result. In most vital matches, fans went into Ibrox knowing that if Cooper could turn it on, their side might win. Of course, no player can be brilliant in every match or even every important one, plus wingers are notoriously inconsistent performers. Even when Cooper did not perform at his best, however, he still fulfilled a function in that the opposing defenders had to make sure that his threat was given due attention and respect, thus making space and maybe opportunities for other Rangers players to do some damage. In some important games, Cooper's very presence was incalculable even if his performance was not.

In his early years at Ibrox, the press dubbed Cooper 'The Moody Blue' due to his apparently shy, taciturn nature that meant he avoided talking to reporters or courting publicity. Too often he came across as a dour, uncooperative type, but his teammates and friends knew that he was just the opposite. Later on, his 'Moody Blue' tag would be gone forever as Cooper grew in confidence, feeling more at ease with the press and showing his true nature. Eventually, he made numerous appearances on television as a pundit, giving viewers valuable insights and charming them with his smile, sense of humour and laid-back personality.

For such a brilliant winger, it is amazing that Cooper only made 22 appearances for Scotland after having been capped first by Jock Stein in a friendly against Peru. It is probably true to say that Cooper's ability, while recognised by various Scotland managers, was grossly under-used. McLeod, Stein, Ferguson and Roxburgh all failed to utilise Cooper properly on the international stage. Inconsistency probably was one of the reasons – a more common problem for international managers who only see their players once in a while. His greatest moment for Scotland was undoubtedly when he equalised with a penalty against Wales in Cardiff to give Scotland a Play-off place in the 1986 World Cup Finals in Mexico. The cool attitude of The Coop was exactly what was needed in that pressure situation when a miss would have been disastrous.

As Graeme Souness continued to bring class players to Ibrox, including great wingers like Mark Walters, Cooper's appearances in the side became more and more sporadic. So, after 12 years with the club, he left for Motherwell, for a fee of £50,000, believing that he still had something to offer a team. His new manager was someone who knew exactly what Cooper could provide for his team – Tommy McLean. An unexpected swansong, however, came in 1991 when Cooper won yet another Scottish Cup-winners' medal in helping 'Well to beat Dundee United in a thrilling Final. It is safe to say that Rangers fans were almost as delighted with the result as 'Well's, thanks to the priceless memories they had of Davie Cooper.

Davie Cooper played 540 games for Rangers and scored 75 goals. He won three League Championships, three Scottish Cups (plus one with Motherwell) and seven League Cups.

## Bobby Russell (1977–86)

The season before Bobby Russell was signed by Jock Wallace, Rangers had won nothing, in contrast to the previous season in which the treble had been achieved. So, many fans were wondering in which direction big Jock's team would take the club. That close season, in addition to Russell, he signed Gordon Smith and Davie Cooper, and when these creative players were added to his existing side a new treble-winning team was born.

Of the newcomers, Russell was the only unknown. The other two, being established pros, cost Rangers relatively big money in transfers. Russell, though, was signed from the ranks of the Juniors – from Shettleston, to be exact. Wallace had been having him watched and eventually gave him a trial. So well did he play that he was signed provisionally and drafted into a reserve match at Tannadice. His display in that game saw him offered a permanent deal at the age of 19.

Jock Wallace saw Russell as his ideal midfield general. The player himself thought that in his first season he would be lucky to get a regular place in the Gers reserve side, but this did not happen. Even he was surprised at the speed of his progress when he was promoted instantly to the first team. Most fans wondered how a player straight from the Juniors could possibly cope with the change to the professionalism of the Premier League, especially such a fragile-looking one. Russell did more than cope. He became a star and justified Wallace's faith in throwing him in at the deep end.

Russell was a player blessed with a natural fitness and had never carried a lot of weight, but he realised that he would have to toughen up. So, in the close season, he spent his time at Ibrox working on his upper-body strength and his core strength. His hard work paid off. Once he started playing, he controlled the midfield like a

Photograph © Action Images / Sporting Pictures / Nick Kidd

(From left to right) Ally McCoist, Bobby Russell and Jimmy Nicholl celebrate with the trophy won at the Skol Cup Final versus Celtic in Hampden Park, 25 March 1984.

veteran. He fitted in perfectly with the established Rangers players and looked like he had played alongside them for years. It was clear to see that he had their respect and that they did not consider him a 'youngster'.

In style, Russell reminded many of the fans of the great Scottish international midfielder John White of Spurs, who died tragically young in a freak lightning accident. Like White, he was frail-looking but had an inner steel, and like the Spurs' legend he was considered a silky, elegant and cultured player. Despite his build, and the knocks he took, Russell could run all day, such was his stamina and fitness. He was not a tackler as such but could take the ball away from an opponent by his sense of anticipation, positioning and stealth. Also, while an attacking midfielder, he could get past opponents without being pacey but by using his body to glide past them almost, reminiscent of Ian McMillan, a Gers hero of the early 1960s. When going forward he showed great vision, an unerring ability to see the simple pass and despatch it at the right time. What made this process easier for him was a brilliant first touch that gave him the necessary time to look around and calculate the most effective pass.

So dominant in midfield did Russell become that fans and pundits alike voiced the view that when Bobby Russell played, Rangers played. Other sides, knowing this, tried to man-mark him, but he either eluded their attentions or this simply gave other great Rangers players the space to capitalise on the situation. For his entire first season Russell played with a skill, determination and graft as well as craft that produced admiration from players and fans of all clubs, such was his impact. At the end of the season Scotland went to the World Cup Finals in Argentina and many fans believed that Russell should have been taken. Manager Ally McLeod obviously thought that, after only one season in the top flight, Russell was too inexperienced and so left him at home. It might have been a lucky escape for Russell, but how Scotland could have used his talents in that competition.

Russell never did get international recognition, due, in part, to a succession of injuries that blighted him and a loss of form at times that probably stemmed from his lengthy spells out injured, especially from a troublesome knee injury. His first season at Ibrox was his finest one, in which he won all three domestic medals and played in 48 of the 53 matches. In terms of appearances, though, the following season was even better in that he played in every competitive Gers game – a grand total of 61. He is still one of the few players to have played in six consecutive Scottish Cup Finals.

Russell was voted Man of the Match in the 1978 Scottish Cup Final when Rangers beat Aberdeen 2–1, and in the 1981 Scottish Cup Final replay (the 'Davie Cooper Final') he scored the second goal in the 4–1 victory over Dundee United. For such a slight player, Russell did have a good shot on him and fired in quite a few from the edge of the box, but his finest, and most important, goal was scored in Eindhoven in a European Cup tie in 1978. With the pulsating second leg tied at 2–2 (after a goalless draw at Ibrox) Russell scored the winner. After a lung-bursting run from his own half, he glided on to an inch-perfect pass from Tommy McLean to slip the ball past the diving PSV 'keeper and clinch the match in the dying minutes. Amazingly, it was his only European goal – but what a goal to remember!

By the arrival of Graeme Souness as manager injuries had taken their toll on the player and the new manager allowed him to be transferred to Motherwell.

Russell played 370 games scored 46 goals. He won one League Championship, three Scottish Cups and four League Cups.

# *Chapter Seven*

# Players Elected Between 1978–86

## History of the Period

With the elevation of captain John Greig to the manager's chair after the surprise and puzzling resignation of Wallace at the end of the treble-winning season of 1977–78, everything still looked to be on track. Rangers, under Greig, were effectively five minutes away from succeeding in back-to-back trebles until a late goal at Celtic Park allowed Celtic to snatch the title and the Ibrox club had to be content with winning the two Cup competitions. From then on, however, it was all downhill, with only the odd League Cup or Scottish Cup win to pacify the fans who were getting more disgruntled as the years wore on, first under Greig, who honourably resigned from his post in 1983, and then again in the second spell of Jock Wallace as the boss.

What was causing even more concern was the fact that Rangers were not even coming in second place to Celtic but were also finishing behind Aberdeen and Dundee United. The nadir for Rangers in the 1970s came in the 1979–80 season when the club finished fifth with a mere 37 points, only winning 15 out of 36 matches and losing almost as many – 14. After that, the best the club could manage was two third places while, by the final few years of the early 1980s, it was a case of finishing fourth or fifth. In the 1985–86 season, the team lost more League games than it had actually won – a unique but unwelcome Rangers record. This was obviously the final straw for the club's board, which sacked Jock Wallace, who had been successor to the failing Greig, and appointed Graeme Souness in an attempt to rejuvenate the entire club.

# MANAGER: JOHN GREIG (1978–83)

The day after Jock Wallace's resignation on 23 May 1978, Rangers made John Greig their next manager. Having been part of three treble-winning Gers teams, captaining two of these, becoming the Scottish Football Writers' Player of the Year for the second time at the end of that season, Greig was a true hero, a legend – Mr Rangers. If any player could make a seamless transition from the dressing room to the manager's office, that man was surely John Greig.

In his favour, he was already respected and admired by directors, players and fans alike. He had served the club for 18 years through the good and the bad times and proved his loyalty throughout. Everybody knew he loved Rangers, was imbued with its traditions, that he had grit, determination and a wealth of domestic and international football experience. He had also observed over the years how other managers had worked at Ibrox, having served under four of them. Plus his experience under international managers would also benefit him. But would all this be enough to become a great Rangers manager?

Sadly, the answer was negative. Rather like Davie White before him, the Ibrox job came too soon for him. Nobody could fault Greig for taking the job as it had probably been his ultimate ambition, but circumstances conspired to thwart his success. His stewardship of the club unfortunately coincided with the rise of Aberdeen and Dundee United, thanks to Alex Ferguson and Jim McLean, not to mention a regeneration of a Billy McNeill-led Celtic. Although he had inherited a treble-winning side, some of those players were past their peak or would be within a season or so. Added to this was the fact that Greig's biggest handicap was his inability to actually replace himself on the field. For so many years, Greig had been every manager's ideal captain, leading by example, showing that never-say-die spirit, shaking his fist at teammates to instil fresh effort or determination into tiring bodies. With Greig now in the boss's seat, that vital influence on the pitch was absent, and in certain games during his first season as manager it showed, to the detriment of Rangers.

The first problem Greig had to solve concerned star striker Derek Johnstone, who had been making noises about wanting a transfer. This was duly done by making the big Dundonian the club captain and moving him back into defence to play at centre-half, as the player had wished. The other favourite Derek, Parlane, would play at centre-forward in place of Johnstone. Apart from a couple of minor players added to the squad, the same players who had won the treble started off Greig's first campaign as manager.

A poor start to the League programme was at least partially offset by a stirring European Cup performance. Greig seemed to have a thoroughness and tactical awareness about him in this environment that surprised a lot of the 'experts' in the game. His first victims in the tournament were Italian champions Juventus, who had half of Italy's World Cup side playing for them. A 1–0 defeat in Turin was overturned at Ibrox with a brilliant, and well-deserved, 2–0 victory. As the competition progressed Greig's Rangers disposed of PSV Eindhoven before taking on Cologne in the quarter-final. Hopes of repeating the Juventus result foundered, though, when, after a similar 1–0 defeat in Germany, Rangers could only draw 1–1 at Ibrox. For a while, however, the new tactically aware Rangers had looked as if they could go all the way in the premier tournament, which was eventually won by Brian Clough's Nottingham Forrest.

Respectability in Europe was also being matched by improved performances at home. Rangers would eventually win both the Scottish Cup, beating Hibs after two replays, and the League Cup, defeating Aberdeen in the Final after having knocked Celtic out in the semi-final. In the League, with three games left, Rangers went to Celtic Park on a Monday evening, knowing that a win would seal the title. Even a draw would probably be enough to take the flag. With Celtic reduced to 10 men and the score 2–2 with only five minutes left, another treble looked to be within Greig's grasp. Then, cruelly an own-goal, followed by a Murdo McLeod thunderbolt, tied up the points and won the Championship for Celtic. Greig, like everybody connected with Rangers, was devastated. Rangers were only a few minutes away from succeeding in back-to-back trebles, a feat that has still never been achieved by any club. It was Rangers' lowest point in that season, but few could have realised then that things were going to get a lot worse under John Greig.

The next season saw Rangers finish fifth in the League, 11 points behind champions Celtic, who also defeated them 1–0 in the Scottish Cup Final. An ageing side, along with injuries and unsuccessful additions to the team, had all played their part in Rangers' demise. Things were scarcely better the following season, 1980–81, but a Scottish Cup triumph after a replay against Dundee United, thanks to Davie Cooper especially, prevented that season from becoming another blank. Over the next two seasons, a solitary League Cup was won and Greig's Rangers were finishing third and fourth in the table far too regularly for the fans' liking. At the start of his final season in charge, Greig had signed the future legend Ally McCoist, but his disappointing start did nothing to help the disastrous beginning to the new season. The signing of McCoist, however, turned out to be Greig's most valuable legacy to the club he loved.

By the end of October, Rangers had already given up on the Championship, having managed to collect a meagre seven points from the first nine matches. A home defeat by a Jock Wallace Motherwell side was the last straw for the loyal fans, who made their feelings known after the match. On 28 October 1983 John Greig, with the interests of Rangers first in his heart, as he always had throughout his career, decided to resign and let another manager try to turn the fortunes of the club around. John Greig won two Scottish Cups and two League Cups.

# Players Elected

## Ally McCoist (1983–98)

Put quite simply, Ally McCoist is the most prolific goalscorer in the history of Rangers. Fifteen years as a Rangers star gave him the platform to achieve his huge number of goals, but who knows what the tally might have been but for a broken leg and the fact that he had turned down Rangers twice before he arrived at Ibrox?

From East Kilbride, Ally had always been a Rangers fan, but when John Greig tried to sign him as a schoolboy, he declined and, instead, found his way into the St Johnstone team in 1978 at the age of 16. A couple of years later and Ally was attracting the attention of bigger clubs by banging in over 20 goals for the Saints. Once again, Greig tried to sign him, but this time it would cost money for the privilege, so £300,000 was offered. Unfortunately for Gers, Sunderland offered £400,000 and Ally was off to Weirside at the age of 18.

Sadly for McCoist, but not for Rangers, his time at Sunderland, a struggling side, was not the happiest on the field. By the summer of 1983, he was ready to come home and John Greig finally signed him for £195,000 – probably the best bit of business Greig ever did for the club as its manager. Despite at last playing for his boyhood club, things did not go as planned in his first two years at Ibrox. Indeed, within less than two seasons, he had been playing under a new manager, Jock

Ally McCoist celebrates after scoring a goal against Dunfermline at East End Park on 28 March 1998.

Wallace, and trying to impress him. Despite a match-winning hat-trick in the 1984 League Cup Final against Celtic, for many months after that McCoist had still to convince the Rangers fans that he was the real McCoy, if not McCoist. He had won over his manager, but many fans remained sceptical.

Ironically, by the time the fans had become worshippers of the man, another manager in the form of Graeme Souness had to be convinced of the striker's worth. By the time of Souness' appointment McCoist had picked up the nickname 'Super Ally' and had been capped for Scotland. He was scoring goals by the barrow-load and, as if that was not enough to make him the fans' hero, he had an engaging personality that perhaps was a factor in his ability to score goals. McCoist was a bubbly, chirpy, extrovert character who always played with a smile on his face. He was always ready to joke with his teammates, opponents and fans alike. If he missed a chance he had the ability to grin and bear it, shrug it aside and be ready to pounce on the next one. He never seemed afraid of missing chances and certainly never hid in a match. An intelligent, educated, witty and articulate man, his press interviews and television appearances merely extended his popularity so that even opposition fans whose team suffered at his hands – or should that be feet? – found him a likeable personality.

Only 5ft 10in tall and weighing 12st, Ally was not a physical forward, although he could handle himself in the penalty box, as all great strikers must be able to do. He was brave, alert, quick off the mark and brilliant at getting into the right place at the right time to finish off moves with a goal. When he scored with his head, it was not the type of soaring header that players like Mark Hateley would later become renowned for. McCoist's headers normally came about because his anticipation and quick reflexes enabled him to get across his marker or in front of him, allowing him the space for a deadly header. Ironically, or perhaps not, as McCoist matured he seemed to score with more headers, and better ones at that!

During his time at Ibrox, McCoist apparently went through over 40 striking partners in the course of breaking his various scoring records. Most would agree, though, that his pairing with Mark Hateley was the most successful one. Having said that, the season before Hateley's arrival McCoist had created a great double act with Mo Johnston. It was in this season, 1989–90, that McCoist broke the Premier Division scoring record and, by scoring two goals in the final Old Firm match of that season, he overtook Derek Johnstone's post-war Rangers record of 132 League goals. This productive partnership, however, was dissolved after a season when Souness decided that the best strike combination for Rangers was one of Hateley and Johnston.

Thus started McCoist's most frustrating time at Ibrox when, with typical humour in the face of adversity, he nicknamed himself 'The Judge', an allusion to all the time he was spending on 'the bench'! At least he had the consolation during this time of knowing that the Gers fans were on his side – and they were letting Graeme Souness know it! When he did come off the bench, McCoist invariably scored a goal and always showed the necessary industry and spirit that would make it harder for his manager to ignore his claims for a starting place. Two fantastic, match-winning goals against Aberdeen at Ibrox were typical of McCoist's substitute performances, nevertheless eliciting no praise from Souness.

When Walter Smith became Rangers' manager, McCoist's fortunes changed once again. Smith decided that a McCoist-Hateley pairing was his preference, and Ally never looked back. He was just about to enjoy the greatest season of his life at that point. In the 1991–92 season he scored 41 goals, which brought him to a career total of 200 for the Scottish League. His spectacular season resulted in him being awarded both the Scottish Sportswriters' and Players' Player of the Year awards, as well as winning the European Golden Boot for being top League scorer throughout Europe. Had he peaked? Not a bit of it! The following season was Rangers' treble campaign, and Ally's goals made a huge contribution to that achievement.

Once again, McCoist won the Golden Boot award with 34 goals in 34 League games, and his total in all competitions was 49. This record was even more remarkable considering the fact that he broke his leg that Spring while playing for Scotland in a World Cup match in Portugal. Who knows how many goals could have been added to his tally if he had played until the end of the season? That injury actually cost him his place in the Scottish Cup-winning side of 1993, which clinched the treble at Parkhead. In fact, the Scottish Cup was never a lucky tournament for Ally, with only one winners' medal to his name. The following season, with Gers

The Golden Boot won by Ally McCoist in 1992 and again in 1993 for being the top League scorer in Europe.

poised to complete back-to-back trebles, McCoist was injured in the warm-up before the Final against Dundee United that Rangers lost 1–0. The presence of Super Ally might just have got Rangers the goal they so desperately needed in that match. In the only other two Rangers Finals after that, McCoist, due to injury, missed out on the 1995–96 5–1 win against Hearts but played in the 1997–98 Final that was won 2–1 by Hearts, his final match for the club.

Even in that last game, the McCoist 'Roy of the Rovers' story might have been repeated for a thrilling finale. With Hearts leading 2–0, McCoist scored, giving Rangers a lifeline with around 10 minutes to get the equaliser. The tide had turned, and it looked like coming. Then, in the final minute, McCoist was fouled right on the 18-yard line after racing through the middle. Everybody, including McCoist, thought that referee Willie Young had given the deserved penalty-kick and Rangers the chance to put the game into extra-time. Imagine the horror when the referee, who had been 20 yards behind the play, awarded a free-kick to Gers – all of one inch outside the box! Thus went Super Ally's last chance to save Rangers with a goal near the end of a game the way he had done in so many matches in the previous 15 years.

Having recovered from that 1993 leg break, he suffered numerous niggling injuries that reduced his appearances in the final seasons of his career at Ibrox. It is fair to say that his total of goals would have been even greater had he played more often in the side that had the genius that was Brian Laudrup creating goals throughout that time. At least he had enjoyed the help of Mark Hateley while banging in all those goals. This partnership, at its peak, was the most prolific in Gers' history. In a two-season spell, especially, they scored over 140 goals between them. Apart from complementing each other in size, ability and style, it was almost as if they had developed a telepathic understanding between them. They might have been the only Rangers strike combination that could arguably have been put in the same class as the Millar and Brand one of the early 1960s.

By the 1995–96 season, McCoist had created a new Rangers scoring record when he surpassed the legendary Bob McPhail's League total of 233 and, although injury restricted his appearances in his veteran seasons, he could still do the business as witnessed when he scored the opening goal against Celtic at Parkhead in a 2–1 Scottish Cup semi-final victory in 1998. For the first half of that season, injury and the incredible scoring exploits of Italian hitman Marco Negri had kept

McCoist out of the side, but when Super Ally had replaced the injured Negri in the new year he scored 16 goals in 26 games. Indeed, his final goal against Celtic saw him equal Jimmy McGrory's Old Firm match total, only surpassed by the feat of Ranger R.C. Hamilton's haul 100 years previously!

By the end of his glittering Rangers career, McCoist had become the club's most prolific striker and one of the greatest characters to have entertained the fans at Ibrox. His smile and celebrations after scoring a goal will never be forgotten. As new manager Dick Advocaat arrived, Ally departed for Kilmarnock, where he played for a couple of seasons when he was not injured. He remains the player with the most Scotland caps (61) while playing for Rangers. In 2007, he returned to Ibrox as assistant to new manager Walter Smith, and Ally's bubbly personality was credited with lifting the low morale of the players and helping to transform the club's fortunes, culminating in regaining the League title in 2009.

Ally McCoist played 581 games for Rangers scoring 355 goals. He won nine League Championships, one Scottish Cup and nine League Cups.

## Ian Durrant (1983–98)

Like his good friend Ally McCoist, Ian Durrant is another character that the Rangers fans will never forget. Like previous Gers legend Alex McDonald, Durrant was born and brought up in the Kinning Park area, near Ibrox, and nobody was left in any doubt that he was a Gers fan who was playing for the jersey. Having come through the schoolboy ranks at Ibrox, it was manager Jock Wallace who gave him his chance in 1985. An energetic, skilful, goalscoring midfield man, Durrant was every manager's dream. He was a lovely passer of the ball, covered every blade of grass like a colt, with his boundless energy and enthusiasm, and had the knack of running ahead of his forwards to get into goalscoring positions. Invariably his technique would see him pass the ball into the net, even from distances of 18 yards and more. Like Alex McDonald in a previous era, Durrant had the innate ability to run on the blind side of defenders and catch them out when the inevitable pass came through to him. Like McCoist, he was a personality who played the game with a smile on his face and who kept morale high in the dressing room with his antics. He was the young player who had the world at his feet, the makings of a Rangers and Scotland legend – and then a dreadful injury changed everything.

In October 1988, at Pittodrie, Aberdeen's Neil Simpson stamped on Durrant's knee and changed the course of his career. As he was carried off, nobody could have known that Durrant would miss virtually the next three seasons, after undergoing various operations in America to repair his shattered knee to enable him to play top-flight football again. In fact, although he did make a comeback, scored more goals and won more medals, even playing 13 times for Scotland, his early promise was never quite fulfilled, although he always remained a hero in the eyes of the Rangers fans.

One of the many reasons for his popularity was his ability to score goals against Celtic. Indeed, he scored against Pat Bonner in his Old Firm debut in November 1985 and enjoyed scoring against Celtic on many other occasions. It was his movement and technique that enabled him to score in so many big games. After his terrible injury, he played a memorable part in Rangers' tremendous Champions League campaign of 1992–93, playing in nine of the 10 unbeaten matches and scoring brilliant goals against Lyngby, Brugge and in Marseille when his equaliser put Gers within another goal of the European Cup Final.

Photograph © Action Images / Sporting Pictures / Tony Marshall

Stuart McCall and Ian Durrant celebrate victory over Aberdeen in the Skol Cup Final at Hampden Park on 25 October 1992.

After that, niggling injuries and new personnel meant that his appearances became less frequent but occasionally still memorable. In fact, in the nine-in-a-row season of 1996–97, he had one last unforgettable part to play in Rangers' history. That March, Rangers travelled to Parkhead to take on Celtic knowing that if they won the game, with so few League matches left afterwards, the ninth consecutive Championship would be theirs. The problem was that the club was suffering an unbelievable injury crisis. So much so that on-loan Welsh 'keeper Andy Dibble had to make his debut and Mark Hateley was re-signed from Queen's Park Rangers especially for the match. When a free-kick was punted from the Gers' half towards the Celtic box, it was Ian Durrant who got away from his marker, got to the ball before the Celtic 'keeper, Kerr, and flicked the ball over him, allowing Laudrup to bundle it in at the goalline. How fitting that the local boy and the legendary foreigner should have combined to virtually tie up nine-in-a-row!

Like most of the great 1990s side, Durrant left Rangers with the arrival of Dick Advocaat and went to play for Kilmarnock for a while before becoming a coach there. All Gers fans wished him the best of luck. He would always be a hero as well as a fan. Then, when Walter Smith returned to Ibrox as manager, bringing with him Ally McCoist, it was not long before Durrant joined them on the coaching staff.

Ian Durrant played 347 games for Rangers and scored 45 goals. He won three League Championships, three Scottish Cups and four League Cups.

# Chapter Eight

# Players Elected Between 1986–91

## History of the Period

This period began with the surprise appointment of Graeme Souness as Rangers' first player-manager and started what must rank as one of the finest eras in the club's history. An Edinburgh man, Souness had had no previous connection with Rangers and, indeed, had never played as a professional in Scotland, having spent all his career in England and Italy; however, the fortunes of the club were at their lowest ebb in its history, so something dramatic was required.

By 1986, the new majority shareholder in the club was Lawrence Malborough, grandson of former chairman John Lawrence. Realising that drastic action had to be taken to restore Rangers to its glory days, he appointed David Holmes as chief executive, giving him a free hand to examine the situation at Ibrox and take the required measures. Holmes' conclusion was that, as a first step, a new manager was required so Jock Wallace would have to go. Following an alarming slump in Rangers' League positions, this, in itself, was not a major shock. His choice of Souness, however, bringing him home from Italian club Sampdoria, was.

Many observers wondered if Souness realised what he was letting himself in for when he accepted the job, but few realised that Holmes would fund any big-money signings that the new manager thought necessary. Rangers was the richest club in Scotland and for too long had not flexed its financial muscles as strongly as it should have. Accordingly, Souness was not so much a breath of fresh air sweeping through the corridors of Ibrox as a hurricane! By the end of his first season in charge, assisted by Walter Smith whom he had lured from Jim McLean at Tannadice, Souness had moved on a total of 15 players, mainly old hands who had outlived their usefulness to the club.

More importantly, in the longer term, Souness' new recruitment policy really revolutionised the whole Scottish game, never mind Rangers. He reversed the age-old trend of Scotland's best players moving to England to better themselves and began to buy English players with a proven pedigree. Various factors played a part in this strategy being successful: Souness' status and reputation in the game (supported by Gers' new determination to pay top wages) and the fact that English clubs were banned at that time from playing in European competitions.

His first signing was Colin West, a barely heard-of English striker, but his next two really made people sit up and take notice at what was happening at Ibrox. First, England 'keeper Chris Woods was signed, followed by England captain Terry Butcher. Later that season, other experienced names such as Graham Roberts and Jimmy Nicholl would follow but, right from the start, the new policy had been set out. England stars such as Ray Wilkins, Trevor Francis and Mark Hateley followed in the seasons to come, alongside Scottish stars such as Mo Johnston and Ian Ferguson, to name but a few. From that first season, with the League title regained, Souness had indeed turned Rangers around.

The next part of the revolution was when the club acquired a new owner. Lawrence Malborough was re-locating to America and looking to sell his majority shareholding. At that time, Souness was a close friend of David Murray, a millionaire Edinburgh businessman. A successful steel magnate, few Scots would have heard of Murray, but once he had bought his stake in Rangers for around £6 million he became a household name and used his expertise in finance to continue the reconstruction of the club with a view to extending its success both on and off the field.

This plan might have faltered near the end of Souness' fourth season as manager when he was tempted away by his old club Liverpool to become its manager, but this did not happen due to the fact that Murray immediately appointed assistant manager Walter Smith as the new boss. Smith brought in his old friend Archie Knox, then assistant to Alex Ferguson at Old Trafford, to be Gers' assistant manager. Together the two oversaw the completion of nine League Championships in a row.

## MANAGER: GRAEME SOUNESS (1986–91)

The appointment of Graeme Souness as Rangers' player-manager in April 1986 astonished all of Scottish football. Souness had had no previous connection with the club, had spent all his professional career outside of Scotland and had no managerial experience. Despite all of this, it was seen as something of a coup for chief executive David Holmes to have lured the man from Sampdoria for a fee of £300,000. Gers might have been getting a novice manager but, in his dual role, they were also getting a classy and experienced midfield player. Many believed that even if the boss's hat did not fit Souness, his ability on the field would pay dividends for the club.

Optimism increased with the news that Dundee United's experienced and much-admired coach Walter Smith would become Souness' assistant manager. Since Souness had little knowledge of the current Scottish game this was seen as a vital move in ensuring that he would settle into his new job with as few errors as possible being committed. Smith, with his wealth of coaching experience, would also be able to deal with the day-to-day training of the players. One of the words commonly used to sum up Souness at that time was 'winner'. He had enjoyed a trophy-laden career at Liverpool, winning all there was to win, including the European Cup, and on the field his desire to succeed showed itself in his crunching tackles and ability to drive his side on. Nobody doubted that the same commitment would be shown in his new role as manager.

Once he had got into his stride as manager, other words would be used to complement that of 'winner' when people were trying to describe his managerial style. Professional, committed, determined, authoritarian, stubborn, abrasive and confrontational were the most frequently used. The players at Ibrox quickly learned that if you did not do things Souness' way, then you would not be around for very long. Having been appointed just before the end of the season, Souness and Smith had the chance to appraise the players they would be taking charge of and decide which would be discarded. With the financial backing of majority shareholder Lawrence Malborough, it quickly became evident that Souness would be spending money, big money in those days, to perform major surgery on the underachieving team.

Souness' intentions were revealed early on when, after signing largely unknown striker Colin West from Watford for £175,000, he secured the services

Player-manager Graeme Souness in 1986.

of England goalkeeper Chris Woods from Norwich for £600,000, then a record for a 'keeper. As if that was not enough, he still had the biggest surprise up his sleeve, and surprising football people seemed to delight Souness. The acquisition of England captain and centre-half Terry Butcher from Ipswich for £725,000 astonished every Scots fan and shocked most English ones. It seemed barely credible that such a high-profile English player would desert England to ply his trade in Scotland. It was to be the start of Souness' policy of signing high-quality players from wherever they played. At a stroke, he had reversed the century-old trend of the best Scots players leaving to 'better' themselves in England. The prestige of Souness, the fact that he had moved to Scotland to play as well as manage, the possibility of European football, the tremendous stadium and the high wages were all factors that lured English players to Ibrox in Souness' early days there.

Souness, like any manager who knows his stuff, realised that a new spine of the side would have to be created and that the defence, especially, would have to be strengthened. Thus, the arrival of Woods, Butcher and West were the first pieces in his jigsaw. He offered £650,000 to Dundee United for their young Scottish defender Richard Gough, whom Souness had played with during the World Cup in Mexico months before, but United refused to sell the player to Rangers and eventually he was sold to Spurs. That season, in December, from Spurs, Souness signed another experienced England defender in Graeme Roberts, but Gough was not forgotten.

As his rookie season started, Souness had cause to feel pleased with the way things had gone. He had secured most of the signings he had wanted and prepared his players well; however, if he had not realised it before, he soon would that every match Rangers play is like a Cup Final for the opposition. Furthermore, Souness' image and his big spending had fostered an even more resentful feeling among some players and managers that meant teams would be getting 'stuck into' Gers as never before. This all kicked-off in the opening League game at Easter Road when a touchy affair had seen Hibs take the lead and a frustrated Souness lash out at George McCluskey. A huge melee took place in the centre circle and, at the end of it, Souness was sent off for his role in sparking off the trouble in the first place. The new Ranger had learned a valuable lesson.

Nevertheless, as Souness learned and his team started to gel, the future looked bright at Ibrox. By October he had won his first trophy by defeating Celtic in the

Skol League Cup Final, and by Christmas they were the League leaders. So strong had Rangers been defensively that a record 12 consecutive clean sheets had been kept by 'keeper Chris Woods until January, when a shock 1–0 Scottish Cup exit at the hands of Hamilton, bottom of the Premier League, broke the sequence. That result was the most disappointing one in the manager's first season in the job, but he kept faith with his players and trusted them to keep up their good work in the League – which they did. In the penultimate League game of the season, at Pittodrie, Rangers only needed a draw to clinch their first Championship in nine years. Unfortunately, the manager was not on the field to see this happen as he had been sent off again in the first half. Fittingly, it was a fierce Terry Butcher header from a Davie Cooper cross (products of the new and old regimes) that had put Gers into the lead and enabled them to hold on for a draw, despite having been reduced to 10 men. How the Rangers fans celebrated when they invaded the Pittodrie pitch and congratulated the players – something that would be unthinkable nowadays.

So, in his first season in management, Souness had regained the title and won the League Cup as well as introducing quality players and instilling a new mood among the players who had already been at the club when he had arrived. The fans had been impressed, as shown by the fact that the average home gate had risen from the previous season's 24,000 to 36,000 for 1986–87. And, remarkably, he had done it all in one season!

Off the field, too, Rangers had started to create policies and sponsorship deals that would increase revenue in order to fund the type of signings that Souness would be aspiring to in the future. Despite such a great start to his managerial career, the next season would let Souness experience the downside of management. Despite acquiring the long-sought-after Richard Gough, Souness' defensive plans were ruined when skipper Terry Butcher broke his leg in November and Gers eventually slumped to third place in the League. Souness had to be content with merely winning the Skol Cup again.

Nevertheless, Souness' exciting signing policy continued unabated, and along with Gough, quality, experienced Englishmen would arrive in the form of Ray Wilkins, Trevor Francis and Mark Walters, as well as Scots such as John Brown. These would be supplemented in his third season by others such as Gary Stevens, Ian Ferguson, Kevin Drinkell and Trevor Steven. This season would see Souness' strongest Rangers side yet regain the Championship and retain the Skol Cup for the third consecutive year. A stunning 5–1 win against old foes Celtic was perhaps the highlight of this season for many Rangers fans. At the start of his stewardship of Rangers, Souness had been of the opinion that a win against Celtic was the same as against any other side, merely gaining two points in the League. By the 5–1 match, however, Souness had come to appreciate the fans' point of view that beating the other half of the Old Firm was not just another victory.

In his fourth season with the club, Souness had his biggest surprise yet for Scottish football fans – apart from his own resignation near the end of the following season, that is. Just before the season started, he shocked just about everybody by signing former Celt Maurice Johnston, who appeared to have signed a contract to re-join his old club. Discovering that the deal was far from done, Souness moved quickly to lure Johnston to Ibrox from his French club, Nantes. What made the whole affair more astonishing to Scots football fans was the fact that, in signing Johnston from under the noses of Celtic, Souness would be breaking with Rangers' unofficial policy of not knowingly signing Catholic players. Johnston became Rangers' first high-profile Catholic player of the modern era, causing more angst among Celtic fans than Gers ones in the process. Souness had stated from the beginning that he would sign players on merit alone regardless of colour or creed, and here he was putting that policy into stunning effect.

This signing paid off handsomely as Johnston scored 19 goals in competitive matches and seemed to complement the striking prowess of Ally McCoist, long the goalscoring hero of Ibrox. Johnston's goals, especially those against Celtic, saw him accepted quickly by the Gers fans, and the future for the striking duo of McCoist and Johnston looked bright. Then, the following season, Souness signed Mark Hateley from Monaco and everything changed. Souness' stubborn streak was emphasised when he decided to pair Hateley with Johnston, leaving McCoist on the bench, to the disgruntlement of the fans. Despite pressure from the fans and sportswriters to re-instate McCoist, the manager kept faith with Hateley, who took quite a while to settle in at Ibrox and win over the fans. Most could see that the big Englishman was the first pick, and the only decision left was whether it would be Johnston or

McCoist to partner him. Few appreciated that it was not Hateley who was keeping their hero out of the side.

In what turned out to be Souness' last season with the club, the Skol Cup was won again after beating Celtic in the Final 2–1, while the League title was retained on the final, thrilling day of the season. By then, however, Souness had gone. With Rangers leading the table from Aberdeen and only four games left, Souness shocked everybody by announcing that he had decided to take the vacant manager's post at his former club, Liverpool. He wanted to see out the League campaign, but chairman David Murray decided that it would be better if he left immediately to let the club concentrate on winning the title. Murray stated that he thought his friend and manager was making the biggest mistake of his career by going to Liverpool, and that he would regret his decision, but he would not stand in his way.

Walter Smith was quickly appointed manager, and when the penultimate match saw Rangers lose at Motherwell it suddenly meant that Rangers had to beat Aberdeen at Ibrox on the final day of the season to win the Championship. Two goals in that game created a new Gers hero in Mark Hateley, and, although Smith was now the manager, every fan knew that it had really been Souness' Championship, his fourth in five seasons.

Souness' departure had shocked Rangers fans as well as most others in Scottish football but, in retrospect, perhaps it should not have been seen as such a stunning course of action. As well as having personal problems in his family life, Souness had incurred the wrath of the SFA, its administrators and Discipline Committee members on more than one occasion, and it was surmised that he felt he was up against it in his dealings with authority. He had also had many confrontations with members of the press and frequently sought out individual reporters when he felt aggrieved at articles they had written. The bitterness of the whole Old Firm sectarian aspect had also depressed him, not to mention being continually under the microscope in such a confined football environment. The lure of restoring the fortunes of the Anfield club no doubt also had a big impact on his decision to leave Rangers.

Whatever his reasons, Souness had left the club in a much healthier state than he had found it, setting it on the road to greater success and, eventually, those nine-in-a-row titles.

Graeme Souness won four League Championships and four League Cups.

# *Players Elected*

## Graeme Souness (1986–91)

When Souness became the Rangers manager in April 1986, many fans were more looking forward to seeing him as a player than a manager. He was the first player-manager in Gers' history, so some wondered if this dual role might adversely affect his playing ability. In truth, perhaps it did, along with various niggling injuries.

Although aged 32 on his arrival at Ibrox, most Gers fans believed that Souness exuded such class and had such an unparalleled experience that he would cruise through the rigours of Scottish football. In a trophy-laden career at Liverpool he had won everything, and then he had gone on to Italy with Sampdoria to further educate himself in the variety of another country's game. Add 54 Scotland caps and participation in three World Cup Finals, and all of this would be put to good use when he started playing for Rangers.

As mentioned above, in his first League game at Easter Road he was sent off following an ugly tackle on McCluskey of Hibs. Later in the season he was ordered off against Celtic and again in the penultimate League match against Aberdeen at Pittodrie, the day his team won the title. Indiscipline such as this saw him fall foul of referees too often, but the situation was not helped by the number of opposition players who seemed determined to mix it with him, rile him and generally wind him up as they looked to take the most high-profile scalp in the game.

Souness at his peak was the perfect midfield 'general'. He was ruthless, powerfully built, had great vision, could spray passes all over the park, was expert at keeping possession, could tackle fiercely and had a tremendous shot on him. His will to win and great drive made him the ideal player to transform the erstwhile ailing Gers side on the park as well as off it. Unfortunately, due to the factors already mentioned, the Rangers fans did not really see the best of him. A succession of injuries took their toll on him, in spite of his being one of the fittest players at Ibrox. He did not really put together a run of consistent great games, but he still had his moments.

One of the most memorable of his displays came in his first Ne'erday match at Ibrox against Celtic which Gers won much more comfortably than the 2–0 scoreline suggested. With the sleet falling intermittently, Souness was at his imperious best. He held the ball up, directed his passes both long and short to either wing and through the middle, regained possession with incisive tackles when necessary and drove his side on to victory, ably abetted by the great Davie Cooper who seemed to thrive on the service he was receiving from his manager. This was a player totally in command of the field. How the Rangers fans adored him for his ability and arrogance. How the Celtic fans must have hated him – for the same reasons!

While that performance was undoubtedly his highwater mark, he did show his skills throughout the season, although he did not dominate entire games the way he had in the Old Firm match. Still, there was always the more ruthless Souness available, ready to put a foot in where angels fear to tread. Many fans can still recall (and probably wince at) the tackle he made on a Steaua Bucharest player at Ibrox in a European Cup quarter-final. It was not the first, or the last, of such tackles in his great career. This fierce, sometimes ruthless, approach to the game, however, sometimes deflected from the brilliant skills that he possessed.

As his managerial career blossomed at Ibrox, his playing career dwindled, helped probably by the better class of player that he had signed for the club. He had less need to use himself in games now that he had such players as Ray Wilkins on the park to do what he used to do supremely well. In truth, Souness is in the Hall of Fame probably more for his feats as a manager than as a Rangers player; although Gers fans were privileged just to see the occasional glimpse of the tremendous player he could be.

Souness played 73 games and scored five goals. He won one League Championship.

## Terry Butcher (1986–90)

When Graeme Souness was appointed as Rangers' player-manager it was seen as a revolutionary step; however, the extent of Souness' proposed revolution only became apparent when he signed England captain Terry Butcher from Ipswich for £750,000. Having already bought England 'keeper Chris Woods, Souness had made Scots fans sit up, but this sensational signing really posted notice that the new Rangers were going for the highest quality of player. Even more surprisingly, despite interest from Manchester United and Spurs, Butcher had committed himself to Rangers, thanks to his admiration for the manager, the stadium he saw, the prospect of European football and, naturally, the excellent salary on offer.

Terry Butcher holding the trophy won at the Skol Cup Final against Celtic on 26 October 1986.

To capture such a player, fresh from starring for England in the 1986 World Cup Finals in Mexico, was not only quite a coup but it also improved the chances of persuading other big names to join the club in the future. Graeme Souness and his assistant Walter Smith had recognised that the defence of the side they were inheriting simply was not good enough, and so their first steps were to rectify that situation and build the spine of a new team. First a new 'keeper had been installed and then came the most important piece of the defensive jigsaw, the centre-half. Terry Butcher was the rock around whom the others could flourish.

At 6ft 4in tall, he really was a rock. A big, brave, powerful 'traditional' centre-half, he had the physical presence to hold a defence together and inspire his teammates. Naturally, he was supreme in the air when defending but was also a great threat to the opposition at corners and free-kicks. His timing and aggression in the tackle made it difficult for forwards to get away from him, and he showed a fleetness of foot that belied his size. Perhaps surprisingly for Scots who had not paid much attention to him while he had been in England, he had a tremendous left foot that could send long, raking, but very accurate, passes up to his forwards. With all those qualities that Souness already admired, Butcher was the obvious choice to be his captain on the field.

The Rangers fans took to the quintessential Englishman from the start, recognising that he was a very good defender but also a player who would give his all for the club. It soon became obvious that he was also a great ambassador for Rangers in the way he conducted himself off the field and dealt comfortably with the media. These communications skills were also put to good use when it came to talking his colleagues through certain games.

Butcher first season went like a dream. Playing consistently well, he inspired his new teammates by leading by example. His will to win was evident, as was the manager's, and this was transferred to all the players. When fellow English international Graham Roberts joined him in the heart of the defence from December, they formed the most formidable barrier in Scottish football. Roberts also had that steel in his make-up and determination to win that meant he fitted in perfectly from the start.

That almost perfect first season ended with Butcher lifting the League Cup after defeating Celtic 2–1 and, his crowning moment at Pittodrie, in May 1987 when his towering header put Rangers into the lead in a game they only had to draw to take the title. This they duly did and nobody was treated as more of a hero by the fans than Terry Butcher. If Butcher's first season had been like a dream, however, his second was a nightmare. Rangers had not started their League campaign well, but in October it plumbed new depths with a 2–2 draw at Ibrox against Celtic. A last-gasp goal by Gough salvaged a point in a match in which Rangers had been trailing 2–0, but it was the discipline aspect that grabbed all the headlines.

In the opening minutes, Gers' 'keeper Chris Woods had been sent off along with Celtic's striker Frank McAvennie for a flare up in the box after the 'keeper had taken possession of the ball. Roberts and Butcher had also been involved but escaped unscathed by the referee. In a way, Roberts' punishment was to be put into goal as no substitute 'keeper was available. The tough central-defender actually did quite well between the sticks, but by half-time Gers were two goals down. Just after half-time, though, Gers had been reduced to nine men when Butcher had been sent off, rather harshly in the view of most Gers fans.

Although goals near the end from McCoist and Gough saw the home side snatch a draw, the furore over the three sendings off was just about to begin. In the end, the Procurator Fiscal intervened, and months later all three who had been sent off ended up in court! A £250 fine was the punishment meted out to Rangers' skipper, but the feeling was that Butcher probably felt that the result of that match had been a bigger punishment to him anyway.

As if all this and trailing Celtic in the League was not enough, Butcher's season was to end in November when he broke his leg in a tackle with Alex McLeish while playing the Dons at Ibrox. With Butcher went any hope Gers had of retaining their title. Significantly, it was the only season in 11 that Rangers failed to take the Championship.

Nevertheless, the following season saw Butcher return and renew what had been his brief partnership with Richard Gough at the heart of the defence. Both men drove the side on to regain the title and almost complete the treble but for a one-goal defeat against Celtic in the Scottish Cup Final. Butcher had an outstanding World Cup for England in Italia 1990, but when he returned he was not quite the same player.

Playing while not fully fit, he looked out of sorts and was not the reliable figure that he has always been until then. Then, in a 2–1 defeat at Tannadice, Butcher scored a spectacular own-goal and was responsible for the other one. It was enough for manager Souness to take drastic action – which he did, dropping his skipper before the Skol League Cup semi-final against Aberdeen in the following game. The captain was furious and had a major row with his manager and stormed off. Not a good idea, as the last player to do that, Graham Roberts, had been shipped out of Ibrox very quickly. Richard Gough was given the captain's armband by Souness, and Butcher's career as a Ranger was virtually at an end.

Wins against Aberdeen and then Celtic in the Final to take the League Cup seemed to justify the manager's decision, but most Rangers fans were disappointed about the way it had all ended. Just over a month later, Butcher was sold to Coventry as player-manager in a £400,000 deal. He may only have spent four seasons as a Gers player, but Terry Butcher had already ensured that he had become a Rangers legend, proven by the fact that he was voted into the greatest-ever Rangers team and is now a member of the Hall of Fame. Apart from his performances, his obvious love for the club and his adopted country have ensured that this proud Englishman will always be considered an honorary Scot by Gers fans everywhere. In 2009 he was the manager of Inverness Caley Thistle and assistant manager of the Scotland team.

Terry Butcher played 176 games for Rangers and scored 11 goals. He won three League Championships and two League Cups.

## Chris Woods (1986–91)

When Souness signed Chris Woods in June 1986, the big English 'keeper was his first high-profile signing. He cost £600,000 from Norwich, but it was not this that made the swoop so sensational. It was the fact that Woods was understudy to Shilton for the England jersey and had played for his country already. In fact, he eventually amassed 43 England caps. For such a player to arrive at Ibrox was bound to cause a stir. Prior to his coming to Ibrox, the 'keeper had won English League Cup medals with both Nottingham Forest and Norwich so this, coupled with his international experience and undoubted talent, made him an ideal selection as Souness started his reconstruction of Rangers from the back.

Woods was big, strong, athletic and commanding. He was agile and a great shot-stopper. He was also probably the best 'keeper Rangers had had for years when it came to dealing with crosses. Rangers, from the start of Woods' tenure, seemed secure at the back. His impact during that first season was there for all to see.

Chris Woods makes a dramatic mid-air catch above the head of Celtic's Brian McClair at Ibrox on 31 August 1986.

Perhaps the best indication came when he set a new British record for shut-outs. Gers had gone 12 matches without conceding a goal – and then Adrian Sprott came along. In a Scottish Cup tie at Ibrox, a mistake by McPherson let the Hamilton Accies player score, giving Woods no chance. So, after 1,196 minutes without conceding a goal the run was over! It is still a British record.

Apart from the shut-out record, one of the other memories of Woods for Gers fans came when he actually stepped up and took a penalty in a European Cup match! In 1990 Rangers were in the process of thrashing Valletta of Malta 10–0 on aggregate when they got a penalty in the 6–0 win at Ibrox. Woods took it and sent the ball low past the post to the ironic cheers of the Rangers fans. An embarrassed Woods trotted back towards his own goal with a rueful smile.

During the 1988–89 season a virus affected Woods that caused him problems with his balance and vision, resulting in him missing much of that season. Even after that had cleared up, he was unlucky in that he was injured at the start of the next season. In the opening match of that season at Ibrox, after the unfurling of the new League flag, disaster struck the 'keeper on what should have been a memorable day. Woods rose for a cross with St Mirren's Kenny McDowell (now, ironically, a Gers coach) and fell awkwardly on his shoulder. The damage kept him out of the team for months. Many Gers fans believed that he was never quite the same 'keeper again after he had recovered from that injury.

When Souness left to manage Liverpool, it was not long before Woods also left Ibrox. It was not so much a change of manager that caused the departure as a change in UEFA rules limiting teams to three foreigners in their competitions. New manager Walter Smith had to address this fact and started by signing Andy Goram from Hibs, who would exceed the exploits of Woods and eventually join him as one of the few 'keepers in the Hall of Fame.

Woods played 230 games and had 119 shut-outs. He won four League Championships and three League Cups.

## Richard Gough (1987–97 & 1997–98)

In 1990, when Graeme Souness eventually sent his erstwhile skipper Terry Butcher to Coventry, perhaps his decision had been made easier by the fact that Butcher's replacement as captain was to be Richard Gough. Like Butcher, Gough was a powerful, inspirational defender who was brilliant in the air at both ends of the

Photograph © Action Images

Captain Richard Gough lifts the Scottish League trophy after the team defeated Dundee United in the Scottish Premier League, May 1993.

Richard Gough's medal collection inside the Ibrox trophy room.

park. In fact, Gough was far more deadly than Butcher when it came to scoring goals. He even managed to score goals with his feet as well as the traditional headers from set pieces.

Born in Stockholm but brought up in South Africa, Gough, thanks to his Scottish father, was eligible to play for Scotland and eventually, before a fall-out with manager Andy Roxburgh, he amassed a total of 61 caps while playing for three different clubs. Gough played at the top with Rangers for another five years after this, so it is fair to claim that, but for his disagreement with Roxburgh, he would have earned the magical 100 caps. When Souness had been appointed Gers manager in 1986, he first got to know Gough better, while both men were on World Cup duty in Mexico. Suitably impressed by Gough's ability and dedication, Souness tried to buy the player from Dundee United, but Jim McLean refused to sell him to Rangers, and eventually he was bought by Spurs and made their captain – quite a testament to how impressed they were with their newcomer.

Souness, however, was a stubborn character and refused to give up on the player he rated so highly for his ability and character. In 1987, Gough became

Rangers' first £1 million signing. At Tannadice, Gough had played mainly as a right-back but, although he started in that position at Ibrox, due to the fact that Butcher was partnered by Graham Roberts at that time, he would soon play in central defence, thanks to Butcher's broken leg that term and the departure of Roberts at the end of that poor season. The following season, Gough was voted Scotland's Player of the Year by the sportswriters, recognising the influence he had exerted on the Rangers side.

Central defence was where Gough's talents were most effective. As stated already, he was supreme in the air but quick and agile on the ground. His tackling was accurate and aggressive, but his marshalling of his defence made sure that the other defenders were alert to any dangers. A model professional, he was a fine athlete and kept himself at the peak of fitness. In fact, most would agree that he was a player who improved with maturity. Plus, he was a figure who inspired those around him by his behaviour on the field, so when Butcher fell out with Souness he was the obvious replacement for the big Englishman in every sense.

This could be seen in his Old Firm debut that was the infamous match when Woods and Butcher had been sent off along with McAvennie of Celtic. Taking over from Terry Butcher, he inspired his eight teammates to hang in when 2–0 down, and with a fierce sense of pride he helped haul the side back into contention. It was fitting that a last-minute equaliser should be prodded into the Celtic net by Gough. In another Old Firm game, the Skol League Cup Final, a month after he had taken over from Butcher, it was Gough who scored the winning goal in extra-time.

These moments should perhaps have been an indication of the type of player and captain Souness had brought to the club. He went on to cement his place as one of Gers' greatest-ever captains, eventually holding the League Championship trophy when nine-in-a-row was completed in 1997, ironically, at Tannadice. Despite being a wonderfully fit athlete, Gough suffered his share of injuries through his career, picking up more as he reached the veteran stage. On more than one occasion, as at Tannadice, when he was presented with the Championship trophy at the end of a game, he would be wearing his suit having missed the match through injury. His bravery and dedication could never be questioned, and fans will remember him playing on in matches with his head bandaged up, a la Terry Butcher for England at that time.

A seemingly cool, unemotional man, Gough touched the hearts of all Rangers fans watching him being presented with the League trophy for nine-in-a-row when his tears showed that the feat meant as much to him as it did to the fans who had been desperate for such an achievement. He had already announced his intention to go to America to play for Kansas City Whiz, but fate played a part in his change of plans. His replacement, Lorenzo Amoruso, was injured before the start of the following season and would not play until the Scottish Cup semi-final at Parkhead in April, so manager Walter Smith sent an SOS to his trusted lieutenant who came back to play one final season at Ibrox. Unfortunately, it did not work out as the team ended with a blank, but it was no fault of Gough who had a fine season personally.

Richard Gough played 427 games for Rangers and scored 34 goals. He won nine League Championships, three Scottish Cups and six League Cups.

## Ray Wilkins (1987–89)

When Souness signed England international Ray Wilkins from Paris St Germain, many pundits and fans thought that he had bought a player who was 'over the hill'. The £250,000 spent on 31-year-old Wilkins, though, turned out to be money well spent. Wilkins by then was a very experienced midfielder who had seen and done it all. He had started his career as a teenage sensation at Chelsea and, in those days, was nicknamed 'Butch' Wilkins. As a man, though, Wilkins could not have been further from the term as he turned out to be a dignified, polite, well-spoken and proper gentleman. No wonder he went on to win 84 caps for his country. He moved from London to Manchester United and later to AC Milan before a career-end move (as many thought) to PSG. Little did they realise that Souness saw him as the ideal player to influence his Rangers side.

In style, Wilkins was a 'midfield general' or what is now termed a 'sitting midfield player'. When he tackled it was by anticipation and timing rather than brute strength. He could intercept or tackle before making space for himself and using his vision to make the correct pass. His greatest asset was his passing. In his career he had been nicknamed 'the crab' by some who obviously were not admirers of his play. They thought that he tended to pass the ball sideways too often, but retaining possession was one of Wilkins' best attributes. He was also capable of brilliant, long, forward passes. In his last game for the club he made

Photograph © Action Images / Sporting Pictures

Ray Wilkins in a battle for possession against Celtic's Billy Stark in the Scottish Premier League at Celtic Park on 20 March 1988.

such a pass to create a goal for Mo Johnston. In a 3–0 win at Ibrox over Motherwell he sent a 50-yard pass right to the feet of 'MoJo', who gleefully smacked the ball into the net. It was a fitting final memory of the man for the Gers fans.

Souness had a great admiration for Wilkins, not only for his style of play, where keeping a cool head and possession was paramount, but also for his personality and influence off the field. He was a dedicated pro who lived properly off the field and who always kept a calm demeanour. As Souness had hoped, he became a great role model for the other Rangers players. His influence in the dressing room was a bonus on top of his playing ability. The tips he picked up from his long career, spanning three countries, from the importance of a proper diet to playing skills, were passed on to younger Gers players like Ian Durrant.

Wilkins may have been a typical Londoner but, like so many others who had not been Gers fans, he came to Ibrox and fell in love with the club. The feeling was mutual. Perhaps Rangers fans' most abiding memory of Ray Wilkins would be the goal he scored in Gers' 5–1 demolition of Celtic at Ibrox in 1988. With Gers having equalised through McCoist, Wilkins set the team off on their brilliant victory when he volleyed a shot into the net from all of 25 yards. It might rank as the greatest goal in his entire career. It certainly left Rangers fans with a delightful memory of a great player.

Wilkins played 96 games and scored three goals. He won two League Championships and one League Cup.

## Ian Ferguson (1988–2000)

As a kid who lived in the East End of Glasgow, a goal-kick away from Parkhead, Ian Ferguson dreamed of scoring against Celtic in the blue of Rangers – and it duly came to pass. In 1991 Ferguson started his professional career at Clyde before moving on to St Mirren for a fee of £60,000. The highlight of his career there, and perhaps one of the highlights of his entire career, was to score the winning goal in the 1987 Scottish Cup Final against Dundee United. That game certainly raised his profile for those who had not already realised that this was an up-and-coming class player.

Graeme Souness knew this already and set out to sign Ferguson for Rangers, but St Mirren, as you would expect, put up stiff resistance to selling their prime asset. The player, who had a stubborn streak in him and was of course a Gers fan, made it clear that he wanted to go to Ibrox. From that point on it was just a question of when and for how much. In February 1988, at 21 years of age, Ferguson signed for Rangers for a fee of £1 million, or just under, depending on which source you believe.

Ferguson was an attacking midfielder who had a great 'engine', could run all day, with a grit and determination that made him the sort of player Souness liked. He was also a strong tackler and could spray a pass around with the bonus of having a fierce shot too. Combine all these qualities with a love for the club and you had the ideal mixture for the manager.

In his first full season he scored the winning goal in the Skol Cup Final against Aberdeen in a 3–2 win, which helped to get the Gers fans on his side early on. The fans always held him in high esteem because they knew that he was a fan himself, playing for the club, and that he would give everything for the team. After his first full season Ferguson was unlucky when it came to injuries and even illness. Various injuries and illnesses meant that for long periods he missed out on the action;

Ian Ferguson holds off Salonika defender Kapetanopoulos in the UEFA Cup second qualifying round at Ibrox Park in Glasgow on 11 August 1998.

however, when he was fit and returned to the side he always made an invaluable contribution. He played nine times for Scotland, and this total would surely have been greater but for his numerous injuries. As for Rangers, most fans believed that he could have had an even more spectacular career if it had not been disrupted so frequently by injury.

Perhaps surprisingly, at the veteran stage of his career, Ferguson survived the Dick Advocaat takeover, and in that manager's first season he was used as a sub on quite a few occasions, including the Old Firm Scottish Cup Final when Gers won 1–0. That was his last big game for the club as he only played another three games the following season. Still, his years at the club, under three different managers, certainly earned him a huge haul in terms of medals – one that few will surpass.

Ferguson played 336 games and scored 46 goals. He won 10 League Championships, three Scottish Cups and five League Cups.

## John Brown (1988–97)

Like the great Bobby Shearer, Brown started as a pro with his hometown team of Hamilton, but unlike Shearer he did not move directly to the team he supported as a boy. It took John Brown quite a while longer to fulfil his dreams. First he moved from Hamilton to Dundee, and then in January 1988 Graeme Souness signed him for Rangers for the bargain sum of £350,000. Brown had come to the attention of Rangers even before Souness' time, though. In 1984, Dundee had knocked Rangers out of the Scottish Cup at Ibrox, with Brown scoring the only goal against his heroes. A year later, he also scored a hat-trick against the Gers, not something that many players have done. And all this from a midfielder at that!

When Brown signed, the cynics claimed that Souness had simply bought him as a squad player, as someone to plug the gaps when injuries took their toll on first picks. But Brown became better than that. He saw off more high-profile defenders such as Basil Boli, Gordan Petric and Dave McPherson in his time at Ibrox.

Brown's versatility was one of his greatest attributes. He could play anywhere along the back four and in midfield. His best position was probably as a central-defender or at left-back, although he could add real bite to midfield when required. He was one of those guys imbued with the 'Rangers spirit', who played for the jersey, who knew what the fans were feeling. A great tackler and good in the air, he could also pass the ball, better than he was often given credit for. A bonus was a powerful shot that was capable

Photograph © Action Images / MSI

John Brown outjumps Kevin McAllister of Hibs in a Scottish League match.

of scoring from 20, or more, yards out. He was one of those players that fans used to describe as 'iron man' of the side. He would have run through a brick wall for the team.

This spirit was best exemplified in the title decider against Aberdeen at Ibrox in 1991. Brown's courage was shown when he took part in that match. He was injured, one of the walking wounded, but so bad was the injury situation before that vital game that he took painkillers to start the match, despite knowing that he might aggravate the injury and perhaps do long-term damage to it. In the second half, having played 60 minutes, he had to be substituted but the game was won by then. No fan will ever forget the sight of Brown at the end of the game 'celebrating' while limping around on crutches. That summed up the guy's spirit.

In Rangers' tremendous treble season of 1993–94, Brown played in 39 of the mammoth 44 League game campaign, all the Cup ties plus 10 European matches. So, he only missed five games in one of Gers' most gruelling and memorable seasons. Not bad for a 'squad player'.

Apart from the sight of Brown hobbling around on crutches, most fans will also remember some of his spectacular goals, like the one he scored against Celtic at

Parkhead in a Ne'er Day derby. With Rangers leading 2–1 and hanging on with only a couple of minutes to go, a breakaway ended with Brown slamming in a 20-odd yarder to finish the game. His joy as he ran behind the goal to salute the Rangers fans reminded them that here was a player who was also a fan – and a great servant to the club.

Brown played 275 games and scored 18 goals. He won six League Championships, three Scottish Cups and three League Cups.

## Mark Hateley (1990–95 & 1997)

In the summer of 1990, Graeme Souness brought Mark Hateley to Ibrox for a fee of £1 million. Despite the fact that Hateley was an English international, had played for AC Milan for four years and was coming from Monaco, it took him some time to win over the Rangers fans. His job was made even more difficult by the fact that the fans perceived, wrongly as it turned out, that he was the player keeping their hero Ally McCoist out of the side. At Monaco, Hateley had been out injured for the best part of 18 months, so the start of his Ibrox career was always going to be hard anyway as he battled to regain his match fitness, touch and goalscoring form. By the end of that first season he had done all of that!

As that season had progressed, the fans had started to see the real value in having Hateley as the team's 'target man', although he was much more than this. He was a big, strong, powerful forward who was marvellous in the air but who had a good first touch and was nimble and quick on the ground for such a big guy. With the hard-working Hateley around, defenders never got a minute's peace as he harried and harassed them for 90 minutes. Goalkeepers, especially, did not enjoy having aerial tussles with him as invariably they came off second best.

By the end of the season Gers fans had started to appreciate the forward but, after the final League game of that season, appreciation had turned to hero worship! Playing Aberdeen at Ibrox, Gers had to beat them to win the title from the Dons. A magnificent first-half header from Hateley set the team on its way, and an early second-half goal from him virtually sealed the match and the title. His Rangers career was truly up and running. As mentioned earlier, when Walter Smith became the manager he paired Hateley with McCoist, and neither player looked back.

The two seemed to get on so well both professionally and personally. Each complemented the other in terms of physique, style and ability. They developed a

Photograph © Action Images

Mark Hateley.

Mark Hateley's England cap, gained by playing against his adopted country.

bond, almost a telepathy that resulted in so many great performances and goals. Hateley's unselfish, combative style set up many a McCoist goal, while Ally's movement and threat also helped Hateley to score so many. In the season when McCoist was absent through having broken his leg, Hateley took on the extra burden of being the side's main goal threat and succeeded, winning the Sportswriters' and the Players' Player of the Year awards at the end of that season. Despite such accolades, he was curiously ignored when it came to being selected for the England team. Puzzled Scots could not understand why such a valuable forward was not being utilised by the Auld Enemy. However, it was England's loss. Despite this, his career total of England caps still came to 32.

Who knows what might have happened if Hateley and McCoist had managed to play together in both the drawn matches in the Champions League against Marseille, the eventual winners? Hateley scored in the first Marseille match at Ibrox that McCoist missed through injury, while in the crucial return game Super Ally played, but Hateley was missing through suspension, having previously been unjustly sent off against Brugge. Morecambe without Wise, Ant without Dec – it just was not the same!

Hateley epitomised the spirit of the great Gers sides of the 1990s. His affectionate nickname was Attila, in homage to the man whose trailing locks accompanied the marauding, deadly performances that were his hallmark. His will to win, his energy, his courage and grit helped Rangers win so many tough games. It was fitting that one of the toughest, the one where nine-in-a-row would virtually be won, should have seen his recall. The season before, he had been sold to Queen's Park Rangers, but in March 1997 Walter Smith brought him back to Rangers in the club's greatest hour of need. As mentioned above, Rangers were scheduled to play Celtic at Parkhead, and it was the Celts' last chance to prevent nine-in-a-row from being won. Rangers were ravaged by injury and needed to show the type of spirit that had seen them get to the brink of nine consecutive Championships. Mark Hateley, more than any player, embodied that spirit. Many saw it as a gamble bringing the 35-year-old striker back, perhaps even just for that one match, but how it paid off!

As he always had done, Hateley rampaged around the park, getting stuck in, upsetting the Celtic defenders and probably terrifying them at the same time. They all knew what a capable striker he could be. For the winning goal, Hateley played his part by jumping up with Celt Annoni for the free-kick punted to the Celtic box.

Both missed the ball, but Hateley's leap had disrupted the Celtic defence enough to allow Durrant to run on to the ball and create the winning goal.

Unfortunately, late in the second half of the fiery match, Hateley was sent off, not for the first time against Celtic, when he clashed with Celtic 'keeper Kerr who had run out of his box to get involved in a flare-up between various players. Gers fans thought that Hateley had been harshly dealt with and that the 'keeper should have been the player to get his marching orders. Nevertheless, the big striker had done his part in the game, ensuring that Rangers took the points and, ultimately, the title. In his next game for Rangers, he ended his Gers scoring exploits by scoring a goal in a 4–0 win against Dunfermline at Ibrox, getting a huge ovation from the Rangers fans who recognised the part he had played in defeating Celtic and ensuring that the dream of nine-in-a-row became reality.

Mark Hateley played 222 games for Rangers and scored 115 goals. He won five League Championships, two Scottish Cups and three League Cups.

# Chapter Nine

# Players Elected Between 1991–98

## History of the Period

Of course, the highlight of this spell was when Rangers equalled Celtic's record of nine-in-a-row League titles in 1997. Conversely, the following season was especially disappointing due to the club's failure to go one better in consecutive titles. Apart from the major disappointment of failing to achieve 10-in-a-row, the other disappointment was in 1993–94 when an unlucky defeat in the Scottish Cup Final prevented the club from winning the treble again. Indeed, this would have seen Rangers win consecutive trebles – a feat still to be achieved by any club. For most Gers fans, though, the complete domination of Old Firm rivals Celtic was the greatest pleasure throughout this period.

In Europe, Rangers' performances still lagged behind domestic ones but, in general, they eventually improved in the European Cup. With Smith as manager, Gers participated in a virtual semi-final in the new-style Champions League when, again, only eventual winners Marseille prevented the club from reaching the Final. Before the advent of the Champions League and its strict seeding, Rangers were unlucky in that they got tough draws in the early rounds of the competition. Since the revamp of the tournament into the Champions League, however, things have been made even tougher for those clubs outside the seeded elite.

### MANAGER: WALTER SMITH (1991–98)
The sudden departure of Graeme Souness may have shocked Scottish football but, for many people, the speedy appointment of Walter Smith as his successor was

equally shocking. After almost five years of big-money signings and glamour, many thought that a big-name manager was what chairman David Murray would be looking for, so the promotion of the assistant manager was indeed a surprise. Those in the know, however, realised that this was a shrewd move from the chairman.

Before joining Rangers, Smith, a Gers fan since boyhood, was recognised as a top-class coach, and throughout the five-year reign of Souness it had been Smith who had had a hands on remit, taking the day-to-day training. The players appreciated him and respected him already. They knew his qualities and that he was capable of stepping into Souness' shoes. Smith had been the perfect foil to Souness in that he was a calming influence, a serious-minded, rational and cool character as opposed to his volcanic boss. Having said that, the players also knew that Smith, while being less confrontational than Souness, was a disciplinarian and no easy touch, soft-spoken though he was.

One of the biggest doubts surrounding the appointment of Smith was whether or not he would have the same influence when it came to attracting the non-Scots players with big reputations to the club. The other doubt was whether he would have the same control and dominance over established international players, without himself having had the kind of playing pedigree that Souness had. Both these doubts were quickly swept aside when it became obvious that Smith had the total respect of all the players and, in time, could still sign top-class players from outside of Scotland.

Having been made manager with only four matches left, with Rangers leading Aberdeen, Smith was expected to complete the job started by Souness and win the Championship; however, as stated earlier, a defeat at Motherwell in the penultimate match meant that Gers had to beat the Dons at Ibrox in the final game to retain their title. With a patched-up side and players who were barely fit enough to finish the crucial 90 minutes, Smith's team won 2–0 thanks to Hateley's goals, and the new manager could breathe a sigh of relief.

When Smith began preparing for his first season in charge, his immediate problem stemmed from rules rather than players. The UEFA 'three foreigners only' rule in European matches had become a big handicap for Rangers, as at that point they had 12 foreign players on the books. Smith realised that he would have to try to decrease the number of foreigners in his squad to compete in Europe while not weakening the side domestically. If only three non-Scots were allowed, then they had to be key men and outfield players, so goalkeeper Chris Woods was the first casualty as Scots 'keeper Andy Goram replaced him. Other Scots who joined were David Robertson and Stuart McCall, both international players. Unfortunately, despite efforts to cope with the three-foreigner rule, Sparta Prague eliminated Rangers from the European Cup in the first round that season on the away goals rule.

Nevertheless, despite failure in Europe, Smith's first season was a successful one as he won the double, a feat Graeme Souness had not been able to manage. Victory over Airdrie in the Scottish Cup Final brought the Cup back to Ibrox for the first time since 1981. Victory over Celtic in the semi-final, when Rangers played most of the match with 10 men, showed the team spirit and skill that Smith's team was infused with. That season paved the way for Smith's most successful one the following year.

The 1992–93 season featured a Gers side at its peak. Not only would Rangers win its fifth title in a row, but the treble would also be achieved for the first time since 1978 under Jock Wallace. Not only that, but Rangers would also sustain their best run in the European Cup since the semi-final appearance in 1960, completing a run of 10 games unbeaten. Just as impressive was the side's 44-match unbeaten run in all competitions.

The most impressive result, and most memorable, was Rangers' elimination of English champions Leeds, with victories home and away, to qualify for the newly-created Champions League. Unfortunately, the one extra goal they needed in a 1–1 draw at Marseille to qualify for the Final eluded them and the fans had to be content with glorious failure in the premier competition. The prolific scoring partnership of McCoist and Hateley played in neither of the Marseille matches as one was missing from each match. Considering the form both players had been in throughout that season, had they played together it might have made all the difference.

Still, domestically it was a wonderful season, with Aberdeen being defeated in the Final of both Cups and yet another title being retained. The one black spot was the broken leg suffered by ace McCoist after he had won the Golden Boot award for being Europe's top scorer, for the second time no less.

Unfortunately, instead of going from strength to strength the following season, it was a relatively disappointing one in that injuries and exhaustion from the previous season's success seemed to take its toll on the squad of players. Nevertheless, the League Cup and the Championship were retained while in the Scottish Cup Final a jaded-looking Gers side went down 1–0 to Dundee United, thereby losing its chance to become the first team in history to win back-to-back trebles.

Still, with the coming seasons, Rangers' success would continue and more brilliant players would be seen in the blue jersey. Perhaps one of the best was Brian Laudrup, who arrived in the summer of 1994. Signed from Fiorentina for £2 million, this Danish winger played the best football of his career at Ibrox. Not only was he thrilling and entertaining to watch, he was also so effective, creating and scoring a lot goals for the team. The following season he was joined by a superstar of a different kind in Paul Gascoigne, the English international whose brilliant performances helped Rangers to win the club's eighth title in a row as well as the Scottish Cup that season.

Despite glittering domestic success, progress in the Champions League still eluded Rangers with the club failing to survive the initial group stage when it did qualify for the competition in the first place. Nevertheless, the greatest moment in the club's history was just around the corner. In the 1996–97 season, Rangers completed the seemingly impossible nine-in-a-row Championships. Smith must be given great credit for the way he kept his side going under the type of pressure that no Scots side had ever had to suffer in the past. Everybody knew that if Rangers failed to win that ninth title, it would seem to many that all those others did not matter at all. Equalling Celtic's record was that important. Despite some nail-biting moments at various points in the season, Smith's Rangers succeeded, and the greatest run in the club's history was completed, ensuring the manager's place in Rangers' folklore.

Unfortunately, the following season was a huge disappointment as departures from Ibrox and injuries to those left meant that the team's effectiveness was reduced. The fact that Walter Smith had intimated that he would resign at the end of that season was seen as another possible reason for the failure of some of the players at the club. The task of achieving 10-in-a-row was also made more difficult by the resurgence of Celtic under a new manager, Wim Jansen. Smith had continued buying star foreign players such as Amoruso, Thern, Porrini and Negri, but the new side failed to make its mark in Europe or to hang on to the League Championship which, near the end of the season, was there for the taking. Defeat in the Scottish Cup Final to Hearts completed a most disappointing final season for Smith as manager. Unfortunately, Smith's team in the 1997–98 season just failed to win the title and create a record 10-in-a-row. Disappointed though the Rangers fans were, they realised how privileged they had been to enjoy such prolonged success under Souness and then Smith, watching brilliant players like Goram, Gough, Gascoigne and Laudrup strut their stuff on the Ibrox turf. Halfway through that season, Walter Smith had intimated to David Murray that he would be resigning at the end of the season so the chairman was given plenty of time to find his replacement. His eventual successor was Dick Advocaat, the manager of PSV Eindhoven.

Walter Smith will always be appreciated for managing the club when it succeeded in winning those nine titles in a row. He guided Rangers to great domestic success, winning the treble and two doubles. He was there when Rangers most needed him, ensuring that, when Graeme Souness suddenly departed, there would be a seamless transition from that regime to Smith's own. He brought some wonderful stars to play for the club and throughout those years gave Rangers fans so much to smile about. True success in Europe never came, but most fans will never forget that tremendous European run of 1993–94 when the Holy Grail of the European Cup was almost within the club's grasp.

Walter Smith won six League Championships, three Scottish Cups and three League Cups.

# Players Elected

## Andy Goram (1991–98)

A year after his arrival at Ibrox, Hateley, one of Gers' greatest strikers, was joined by the club's greatest-ever goalkeeper, Andy Goram. Over the coming years, while one was banging in goals at one end, the other was saving them at the other. Lancashire lad Goram had started out playing between the sticks for Oldham and, thanks to a Scottish grandparent, even gained his first Scottish cap while playing for them. He would eventually make another 42 appearances for Scotland. A move from Oldham to Hibs saw him spend the next four seasons there until Walter Smith signed him to replace Chris Woods, a victim of UEFA's 'three foreigner only' rule in those days.

Andy Goram celebrates with the trophy won in the Scottish Coca Cola League Cup against Hearts at Celtic Park on 24 November 1996.

It certainly was a case of being in the right place at the right time. And Goram would continue being in the right place at the right time while guarding the Gers goal. His saves and personality made him a Rangers legend who was voted Rangers' greatest 'keeper by the fans and was elected to the Hall of Fame.

Bearing these accolades in mind, it is ironic that his start at Ibrox was inauspicious, to say the least. In an early League game at Tynecastle, he was at fault for letting in the only goal of the game as he watched a long-range effort that looked to be going past slam into his goal. Then, even worse followed a month later when he should have saved the away goal scored by Sparta Prague at Ibrox that put Rangers out of the European Cup; however, despite those disappointments, Goram drew strength from them and soon had the fans convinced that he was worthy of taking over from Chris Woods who had been Rangers' best 'keeper in a generation.

At only 5ft 11in tall, Goram was relatively small for a goalkeeper, but his sturdy build meant that he could take care of himself in a crowded penalty box. Due to his size, he stayed on his line when crosses were put in more than most 'keepers, and when he did come for a cross his favoured method of dealing with them was to punch the ball away to safety. If this was a handicap, it never seemed like that to the fans who could only admire him for all his other qualities.

Goram was quick on his feet, with the quick reflexes that any top 'keeper must have. His confidence spread itself to the rest of his defence, and the defenders must have felt safe in the knowledge that he was behind them should a forward break through. This was perhaps where Goram was seen at his best. In a one-on-one situation, he would stay on his feet, making himself look as big as possible to the onrushing forward and making him decide how he was going to get the ball past him. Invariably the striker did not! A dive at the forward's feet, an outstretched palm, a leg in the way – the ball stayed out one way or another. By the time he had established his reputation, he must have held a psychological edge over any striker bearing down on his goal.

The 1992–93 season was probably his finest. In that treble-winning season, Rangers enjoyed a 44-game unbeaten run and almost made it to the Final of the first Champions League. Goram was instrumental in all of that, playing brilliantly in those European matches and especially against Leeds at Elland Road. Domestically, he was practically unbeatable, keeping 25 clean sheets that season.

Not surprisingly, he was named as the Sportswriters' Player of the Year. A knee injury ruined the following season for him, and it is fair to surmise that Rangers might have completed back-to-back trebles if Goram had played in the Scottish Cup Final when a mix up between David McPherson and substitute 'keeper Ally Maxwell caused the solitary goal that gave the trophy to Dundee United.

Once he started to pick up injuries and had problems with his knees, his fitness suffered, and he had a tendency to put on weight that led to some fans nicknaming him 'The Flying Pig'. It did not seem to influence his effectiveness, though, as he was adored by the fans. Still, at one point in his Ibrox career, Walter Smith was so disappointed in Goram's physical condition that he put him on the transfer list. This gave him enough of a fright to get back to peak conditioning so that his performances improved and returned to their former level.

The only people disappointed by that were probably Celtic fans and, in particular, Celts' manager Tommy Burns. This was because it almost seemed that Goram saved his most stupendous performances for Old Firm matches. Time and again, when Gers were on the rack, especially in games at Parkhead, Goram would pull off unbelievable saves that would inspire his teammates and deflate the opposition. Invariably he would keep his side in the game until a Gers forward would score a goal and snatch the points. Then, it was almost as if the Celtic players knew that they would never get the ball past Goram. Tommy Burns once summed up his frustration and admiration for Goram's abilities when he said, 'When I die, they will put on my tombstone, "Andy Goram broke his heart".'

If 1992–93 was Goram's greatest season, few would disagree that his greatest single save came in an Old Firm match at Ibrox in November 1995. In a marvellous League match that ended 3–3, with the game ebbing and flowing, ace Celtic striker Van Hooijdonk, from a couple of yards out, volleyed a cross goalwards. Never was Goram's anticipation and quickness of foot seen better than in the way he got across his goalline to somehow paw the ball away when the thousands of Celtic fans behind him were jumping up to celebrate a goal.

Such saves live in the memory forever. It was saves like this that earned Goram his nickname of 'The Goalie' – a simple nickname that somehow said it all about the way the Rangers fans felt about Andy Goram.

Andy Goram played 258 games for the club. He won five League Championships, three Scottish Cups and two League Cups.

## Stuart McCall (1991–98)

One of the most amazing aspects of Stuart McCall's affinity with the club was that, although a Scottish international, he was born in Leeds and his accent was as Yorkshire as they come. His father was a Scot so that is how he qualified to star for Scotland and eventually win 40 caps.

His first football love was Bradford, and he had the misfortune to be on the pitch that dreadful day of the Valley Parade fire which killed so many. With true Yorkshire (and Scottish) grit, McCall moved on to forge a career for himself despite that traumatic event. He was transferred to Everton and played in the FA Cup Final of 1989 against Liverpool, just after the Hillsborough Disaster. Although Everton lost 3–2, it was McCall who scored both their goals.

In August 1991, McCall became one of Walter Smith's first signings when he was bought for £1.2 million. In his European home debut against Sparta Prague he actually scored Gers' two goals, but at the other end another debutant, Andy Goram, let one in to see Gers eliminated on the away goals rule. Afterwards, McCall stated

Stuart McCall being persued by Donnelly and O'Neill of Celtic on 28 September 1996.

that he hoped that the Gers fans did not think that it was 'normal' for him to be scoring goals, as it was not something that he was prolific in.

McCall was a modern midfielder with great energy, drive and spirit. He seemed to be tireless and covered every blade of grass for the full 90 minutes. He had not only the physical attributes to prosper in the Premier League but the correct mentality as well. He had that never-say-die attitude which became invaluable. Although not a tall player, he was a fierce competitor, and his tenacious tackling could take care of opponents much bigger than himself. He was also quick and had a footballing brain that enabled him to make space for himself and sent off great passes to set up attacks. He also showed a great willingness and ability to track back and put in some saving tackles when necessary.

With such a whole-hearted player it is almost inevitable that injury would interrupt his career and it duly did. Twice he needed surgery, but each time he came back with the same spirit and energy. He was the type of player that every great team needs, and Rangers were lucky to have him to help them on the way to nine-in-a-row titles.

When Walter Smith left Ibrox so too did McCall, and he returned to his first love, Bradford – where else? As befitting such a super-fit and dedicated pro, he played on until he was 40. He is currently that club's manager.

McCall played 264 games and scored 20 goals. He won five League Championships, three Scottish Cups and two League Cups.

## Brian Laudrup (1994–98)

To show the esteem in which Brian Laudrup is held by Rangers fans, you need only remember that he is the only foreign player to have been voted into the greatest-ever Rangers team. Before arriving at Ibrox, Laudrup had played in his native Denmark, Germany and Italy, so he was an experienced campaigner, but the fee of £2.5 million paid to Fiorentina was to become one of the greatest bargains in Gers' history as the Dane went on to play the best football of his career at Ibrox.

To describe Laudrup as a tremendous left-winger is simply inadequate. He was so much more than a winger. A natural athlete, he was hard-working and dedicated, plus he had all those qualities in a forward that simply terrify defenders. Pace, terrific acceleration and sublime ball control coupled with vision made him a nightmare to play against and a joy for Rangers fans to watch. Having said that, at

Brian Laudrup is tackled by Mike Galloway of Celtic on 27 August 1994.

almost 6ft tall he was not in the mould of the traditional Rangers 'tanner ba' winger. He was the sophisticated modern version of it. With Laudrup in the side, Gers fans thought that it was possible for their team to beat anybody. Not only was he a productive player, setting up chances for his teammates with quality crosses and cut-backs and scoring fantastic goals himself, but he was also an entertainer. The fans just loved watching him run at the opposition and bamboozling defenders with his skill and speed. A mazy dribble from Laudrup was something to live in the memory.

Laudrup's ability to twist and turn might have been a great asset, but so was his coolness under pressure. Even in the penalty area it always looked as if his control and intelligence gave him that extra edge in finding space or a colleague to pass to. When he raced infield, waltzing past one defender after another, it must have been a sobering sight to the opposition, knowing that, at any time, he could unleash a powerful shot that would be unstoppable. No wonder he ended up with 82 caps for Denmark.

In an Ibrox career of many highs, perhaps two especially should be identified. His most memorable performance must be the Scottish Cup Final of 1996 at Hampden when, almost single-handedly, he destroyed Hearts. Not only did he score two of the five goals that day, but he also set up the others that constituted Gordon Durie's hat-trick. Normally, a hat-trick in a Final would see that player named man of the match, but in that game it was the genius of Laudrup that had lit up the old stadium. The words 'Laudrup's Final' would bring back happy memories to any Rangers fan in years to come.

If that match saw Laudrup's greatest performance, then his most memorable and important goal was seen the following season at Tannadice when, ironically, it was a goal from Laudrup's head, rather than either talented foot, that ensured Rangers won their ninth consecutive Championship that night. Headers were one of his few weaknesses, but he bulleted that one in as if he were Mark Hateley! That goal might have been the most significant in his Ibrox career, but there were so many others.

Laudrup was a curse to Celtic in his time with Rangers, scoring quite a few memorable goals in League matches at Ibrox, Parkhead and, in the League and Scottish Cup, at Hampden. As Celtic's O'Neill discovered one night at Parkhead, one slip against the man could be costly. With the score 0–0, O'Neill slipped as he tried to control the ball in the centre of the park, just inside his own half. Laudrup pounced on it and raced away from the defence, straight up the middle. Then, from 18 yards out he smashed the ball into the net for the goal that would win the points that night.

In his four seasons at Ibrox, Laudrup won the Sportswriters' Player of the Year award twice, in 1995 and 1997. In the other two seasons he was plagued by niggling injuries that caused him to miss quite a few matches. Besides, the season between his two awards saw the accolade going to his teammate Paul Gascoigne, whose performances had been stunning, so he had no need to feel disappointed. At the end of his third season, he changed his mind about leaving Rangers to go to Ajax and stayed for another season, but even the brilliant Dane could not inspire a jaded Rangers side to capture the longed-for 10-in-a-row. At the end of that season, he signed for Chelsea but left behind some golden memories of one of the most skilful players ever to have worn the blue jersey.

Brian Laudrup played 150 games and scored 44 goals. He won three League Championships, one Scottish Cup and one League Cup.

# Paul Gascoigne (1995–98)

When Rangers signed 'Gazza' in the summer of 1995 from Lazio for a fee of £4.3 million, it was probably the biggest coup ever seen in Scottish football. Here was the English hero of Italia '90 and the midfielder acknowledged by English fans as the most talented player of his generation coming to Scotland – and he was not even at the veteran stage yet! Rangers knew they were getting a world-class performer to join their other one, Laudrup, but manager Smith also knew that the two players were chalk and cheese when it came to their personality. Gascoigne brought genius and madness with him as well as a lot of baggage for the media to latch onto, whereas Laudrup was the model professional with a stable and happy home life.

In Italy, injury and the alien football culture had caused Gascoigne's career to stall somewhat so he was ready for returning home. Few could have suspected that 'home' would turn out to be Govan! From his arrival at the stadium, Gazza captured the hearts of the Gers fans and fired their imagination. Before a ball had been kicked, young fans were copying his hairstyle and getting their hair dyed blond like his, much to the despair of their mothers, no doubt. His cheeky, happy-go-lucky persona made him an attractive new hero for the fans to worship, but it was on the field that his talent generated most admiration.

A modern midfield player, Gascoigne combined strength with skill. His surging runs created many a goal, sometimes scored by himself. He showed great vision and had a variety of passing skills that meant he could open up defences at will. Excellent ball control and an instant first touch gave him the time and space to set off on a penetrating run that sometimes became almost a mazy dribble through the opposition. He used his upper body strength to ward off any challenges and sometimes, too, his elbows – a tactic that caused some controversy at times. A genuine, goalscoring, creative midfield player who got himself ahead of forwards into scoring positions, Gascoigne was very difficult to mark. No wonder he eventually amassed 57 caps for England.

Gascoigne's greatest weakness was his discipline. A tendency to retaliate against opponents who spent the whole match trying to stop him illegally and a penchant for dissent made referees show him the yellow card too easily. Famously, one even booked him once when he had dropped a yellow card that was later picked up by Gazza. As the player returned it to the ref, jokingly pretending to book him, the ref

Paul Gascoigne celebrates his goal versus Steaua Bucharest in the European Champions League on 22 November 1995.

called him back and showed him the yellow card for real! To his credit, Gascoigne merely smiled at the official as he walked away with yet another unjust booking.

Gascoigne's first season at Ibrox was simply sensational. He thrilled and entertained the fans, caused all sorts of controversy, basically won the match for Rangers that sealed the title and won the Sportswriters' Player of the Year award. In fact, the entertainment and controversy started with a pre-season friendly against Steaua Bucharest when, after it had been suggested by Ian Ferguson beforehand as a celebration, he scored a goal and pretended to play the flute in front of the Gers fans at Ibrox. Cue condemnation from the media in the Sunday papers next day. The Englishman had a lot to learn about football politics in Scotland. Although he eventually did get clued up, it did not ever curb his mischievous and controversial behaviour both on and off the field.

Throughout his first season, Gascoigne's brand of football magic and fun lit up Ibrox and the other stadia of Scotland. He controlled matches, set up goals and scored some memorable ones himself in that time. Space does not permit the detail needed to thoroughly capture his achievements during that season; however, even some snapshots of his deeds might just bring back wonderful memories of the fans who witnessed his exploits.

In his first Old Firm League game at Parkhead, he scored a brilliant second goal in Gers' 2–0 win. With the ball in the Rangers box, it was cleared upfield to Salenko on the halfway line. He passed it out to the right for McCoist to run on to, and his pass into the centre was reached by Gascoigne who had started his run from his own penalty area when the ball had originally been cleared. How he got from one end to the other in a few seconds defied belief. Not only that, but he controlled the ball and coolly dispatched it to the side of the 'keeper, Marshall.

In the crunch match at Ibrox against Aberdeen, when a Gers win would seal the title, Rangers were a goal down before Gazza took on the Dons' defence single-handedly to equalise before half-time. A penalty and another stunning goal gave Rangers the necessary victory and eight-in-a-row. His second goal will never be forgotten by fans who were there that day. Collecting the ball deep in his own half, he went on one of those characteristic, lung-bursting runs of his. Straight through the centre of the Dons' defence he ran, shaking off one opponent after another before passing a shot into the corner of the net.

As often as not, his great technique saw Gascoigne passing the ball into the goal rather than blasting it. This was seen at its best in the following season's League Cup Final at Parkhead against Hearts, who had come from two goals behind to equalise in the second half. With Rangers looking for inspiration, it was Gazza at his best who provided it. His two goals exemplified his movement, vision and skill perfectly as he passed the ball into the net once he had made the space to try it.

In a League match at Ibrox against Celtic, with a couple of minutes left and Gers leading 1–0, a Celtic header smacked off the bar. The ball was swept up the field quickly in a series of quick passes and when Albertz curled a lovely cross into the box from the left, there was Gazza diving in, to head it into the net and seal a Rangers win. As usual, he had run the length of the pitch to finish off the move.

In a League game that season at Ibrox against Hibs, Rangers thrashed the visitors 7–1, and although Durie scored four of the goals it was Gazza's that fans remembered. Picking the ball up just inside the Hibs half, he went on a mazy dribble, waltzing past five Hibs players before tucking the ball away confidently. Such solo efforts were not unusual. In fact they were his trademark. With a genius like Gascoigne in the team, anything was possible.

Unfortunately, Gascoigne's playing rhythm and form was interrupted all too frequently in the latter part of his second season by injury and suspension. Having said that, he was part of the side that won nine-in-a-row that memorable evening at Tannadice. Although he still scored unforgettable goals and gave performances that were out of this world, they became less frequent. With a loss of form and personal problems piling up, he was allowed to leave the club for £3.5 million to Middlesbrough before the end of a season that saw the club fail in its quest for 10-in-a-row. Many Gers fans believed that letting him leave when he did reduced the chances of a Gers title win that season.

Gazza was gone but the memory lingered. He was, and still is, a Rangers hero, rightfully taking his place in the greatest-ever Rangers team and in the Hall of Fame.

Paul Gascoigne played 103 games and scored 39 goals. He won two League Championships, one Scottish Cup and one League Cup.

## Jorg Albertz (1996–2001)

In an era when many foreign players came to Ibrox, played and left, German midfielder Albertz came, played and conquered. He was elected to Rangers' Hall of

Fame, a distinction he shares with its other foreign Rangers, Brian Laudrup and Stefan Klos. Albertz generated many wonderful memories of spectacular and crucial goals scored. He became an adopted Scot and the Gers fans took him to their hearts.

An unknown in this country, when he was signed in 1996 by Walter Smith for £4 million from Hamburg, Jorg Albertz quickly made his mark with his explosive shooting power that thrilled the fans from his earliest days at Ibrox. Never was a nickname so appropriate – 'The Hammer'. His relationship with the fans was cemented by his obvious love for the club, his 100 per cent commitment and the enjoyment he showed while playing.

By the time of the crucial Ne'er Day Old Firm game at Ibrox in his first season, he had already become a firm favourite with the Gers fans, but his esteem soared with the free-kick he blasted past Celts 'keeper Kerr from 25 yards. The net-bound ball apparently travelled at almost 80mph while on its way to give the home side the lead. Such strikes were not unusual. Albertz goals were normally spectacular, whether from dead ball situations or open play.

A big, strapping midfield man at 6ft 2in, Albertz was not cumbersome nor was he a one-trick pony. He worked tirelessly, covering the park from one end to the other, could tackle and win the ball but also had a sublime passing skill that could feed a winger or spray passes to the other side of the field. Many a goal was also scored from a curling, accurate Albertz cross. His general link play, attacking threat and goals scored contributed to the Gers' title win that brought about nine-in-a-row. But if that moment was his proudest, then the following season was his most disappointing.

Despite scoring two unforgettably brilliant solo goals in seven days against Celtic at Parkhead in a Scottish Cup semi-final and at Ibrox in the League, putting his side top of the table, his efforts were to no avail. Rangers threw away the chance for their 10th consecutive title in the few matches remaining, and Albertz was harshly sent off in the League match the week before the Cup Final against Hearts, thereby being suspended and unable to help Gers salvage a trophy that season.

Despite that, Albertz had performed very well in both his seasons at Ibrox, so it was no surprise that when new manager Dick Advocaat took over, the big German was one of the few stars that he had decided to keep while building his new Rangers. In that initial Advocaat season of 1998–99, Albertz continued where he had left off, scoring brilliant goals and endearing himself to the Rangers fans. While on the way

Jorg Albertz raises the trophy won at the Scottish League Cup Final versus St. Johnstone on 29 November 1998 at Celtic Park.

to another treble, his goals entertained the fans, and he shone in a midfield that contained Barry Ferguson and Giovanni van Bronckhorst – no mean feat! He was by far the most productive midfielder in terms of scoring goals and, indeed, in one match, against Dundee at Ibrox that February, he scored a stunning hat-trick, something that no other Gers player managed that season.

The following season was another vintage one, with great performances and goals against the likes of PSV in Holland and Aberdeen in the Scottish Cup Final, when his 30-yard free-kick practically shattered the Hampden woodwork before going over the line, followed by Wallace and McCann. The double was completed and, as usual, Albertz had played his part in that achievement.

Despite constant rumours that the German did not always see eye to eye with his manager, Albertz seemed a permanent fixture; however, the following season saw him miss more and more games due to a succession of injuries. Nevertheless, he came back before the end of the season and even won a Player of the Month award, but his fate had already been decided by Advocaat. His final League game was against Hibs at Ibrox, where the fans cheered him off the park, knowing that he was on his way back to Hamburg.

Jorg Albertz played 182 games for Rangers and scored 82 goals. He won three League Championships, one Scottish Cup and two League Cups.

## Barry Ferguson (1996–2003 & 2005–2009)

When he signed from Rangers Boys Club, Barry Ferguson was not only a Rangers fan but also a younger brother of a previous Gers player, Derek, who had starred for the club in the 1980s. He made his first-team debut at the age of 19 in the 1996–97 season, when he played in the final, meaningless, fixture at Tynecastle with the title already having been won three days earlier. So, technically, Ferguson was part of the squad of players who won nine-in-a-row.

It was the following season, however, that manager Walter Smith started to play him in more games, to the delight of the crowd that could see they were watching a special talent in midfield. To the fans' disappointment, though, due to injury and loss of form the youngster only played 11 matches as the manager tried to ensure that he did not suffer from burn out later on in the campaign.

With the arrival of new manager Dick Advocaat, however, things changed dramatically for Ferguson, who had been harbouring thoughts of having to move on to another club to further his experience of first-team football. The Dutch coach, observing the team in the months before taking over, had realised that Ferguson could be a great playmaker in his new midfield, and so when he arrived he made this clear to the player and anyone else who cared to listen. His faith in Ferguson inspired him to produce a series of outstanding displays, which meant he was considered a regular in the side and an established talent.

In that first season, when the treble was won, Ferguson was immense. Fit, enthusiastic and determined, he gave his all for the team. He was a midfielder whose desire shone through and was accompanied by the vision and passing skills to make him an invaluable member of the side. He chased and tackled the opposition when they had the ball and set up attacks when Rangers had it. The one disappointment for the player that season was that, due to injury, he missed out on the Scottish Cup Final win against Celtic that clinched the treble. Perhaps he would not have minded so much if someone could have told him that within four years he would be captaining Rangers to another treble.

In his first two seasons playing for Rangers in Europe he also made a big impact with his displays against various teams. So much so that Bayer Leverkusen manager Christophe Daum valued him at £10 million even before he destroyed them in Germany. Free of injury, his performances at home got better and better too, and it was obvious that Rangers had found the new midfield general they needed among a squad of midfielders that consisted of great players such as Albertz, van Bronckhorst, Tugay and Reyna.

When Dick Advocaat decided to take the captain's armband from Lorenzo Amoruso following a disappointing lapse in a European match, he surprised everybody by making Ferguson the skipper. Many thought that Ferguson was too young for the burden of such an honour, but Advocaat was proved correct as the youngster grew in the job and led his side by example, showing the traditional Rangers spirit that brought the side back from the brink on many an occasion. He became the youngest player ever to captain Rangers to a treble victory.

Throughout his time at Ibrox there were only two evident weaknesses in Ferguson's game. One was his discipline that saw him sent off three times, once at Parkhead. This usually came about because of his passion for the club, his enthusiasm and his frustration when things were going badly – not that that happened too often initially. The other weakness had been his scoring record for a

Barry Ferguson celebrates winning the CIS Insurance Cup Final versus Dundee United at Hampden Park on 16 March 2008.

midfield man. Hard work, coaching and practice, however, rectified this during the 2002–03 season, when his haul of 18 goals contributed greatly to Rangers' treble success.

Those goals were a mixture of penalties, free-kicks and goals from open play. His free-kicks had improved so much that when one was awarded within 25 yards of goal, Gers fans expected his effort to be on target, if not in the net. It was such a free-kick that equalised in the 2002 Scottish Cup Final against Celtic in what many believe was Ferguson's finest game. In that match, he had shown all his skills but just as important his grit and energy to ensure that Rangers came from behind to deservedly take the Cup with a last-minute Lovenkrands goal.

Ferguson's runs into the opposition box improved considerably the following season so that some wonderful goals were the end product of his ability to start a move and then follow it up by reaching the danger area to finish it off. One memorable goal that stands out as an example of this was at Tannadice, when Ferguson sent a long, raking pass from his own half for Ronald de Boer to run on to and catch at the opposition goalline. After controlling the ball and looking up, de Boer threaded his pass into the box where Ferguson, who had run half the length of the park, met it and crashed a brilliant shot into the roof of the net. It was goals like this that showed the improvement in Ferguson's play as he had matured into a classy midfield maestro. The 21 appearances he made for Scotland, which would have been more but for injury, also proved how great a player he had become. At the time of writing he has now played 44 times for his country.

Just before the start of the 2003–04 season, Ferguson shocked everybody at Ibrox by requesting a transfer. He stated that he wanted to try his luck in England and meet new challenges. No amount of persuasion by Rangers manager Alex McLeish or the chairman, John McClelland, could make him change his mind. Therefore, a bid of £7.25 million from Blackburn was accepted and he went to Lancashire to join former Gers manager Graeme Souness' club.

However, 18 months later he returned to the club he loved, despite having been successful at Blackburn and becoming their captain. A serious knee injury had curtailed his career there and perhaps influenced his desire to return to Rangers. His presence in midfield no doubt helped the Gers win the 2005 title. In 2006, at the age of only 28, Ferguson was awarded the M.B.E., joining John Greig, Walter Smith and Ally McCoist as Rangers who have been honoured by Her Majesty. Also, he has been awarded the Sportswriters' Player of the Year award twice. In the 2007–08 season he led Rangers to victory in the two domestic Cup competitions and became only the third Ranger to captain a side in the Final of a European competition when he led the team out at The City of Manchester Stadium to play Zenit St Petersburg in the 2008 Final of the UEFA Cup. That European campaign saw Ferguson become the scot with the most appearances in European club competition. He broke Dundee United's David Narey's total when he played his 77th match at Ibrox against Werder Bremen. By the end of that season Ferguson had competed in 82 European matches.

The following season was most disappointing in that, due to injury, he was absent for the first four months and, when he returned to the team, found it difficult to recapture his form. Even worse, in March 2009 he was suspended indefinitely by the Scottish Football Association following an incident of indiscipline while at the Scotland team's headquarters between World Cup games against Holland and Iceland. As a further consequence, Rangers manager Walter Smith suspended Ferguson from the club for two weeks. Happily, though, he played in the title-winning game at Tannadice and the Scottish Cup Final win against Falkirk at Hampden a week later. On 17 July 2009 Ferguson was transferred to newly promoted Birmingham City on a three-year contract for just over £1 million.

Barry Ferguson has played a total of 423 games for Rangers and has scored 60 goals. He has won five League Championships, five Scottish Cups and five League Cups.

# Chapter Ten

# Players Elected Between 1998–2001

---

## History of the Period

Halfway through the 1997–98 season, manager Walter Smith announced his intention to leave Ibrox at the end of that season, regardless of whether Rangers achieved the coveted 10-in-a-row League titles. As it turned out, Rangers finished the season trophyless. Chairman David Murray had discovered his new manager months before when he signed up PSV manager Dick Advocaat. That gave Gers' first foreign manager plenty of time to assess his squad and target new players to be introduced. In the end, most of the veteran Gers players were moved on and virtually a new team was assembled at enormous expense.

Many Rangers fans were dubious about having a foreign manager and wondered whether a completely new side could gel quickly enough to wrest the title back from Celtic at the first attempt. Advocaat not only did that, but he also won Rangers' sixth treble in the process. The following season the double was won, and throughout it all Gers were playing a brand of attacking football that had the fans in raptures.

Perhaps the most pleasing aspect of Advocaat's tenure was the great improvement in the side's European displays. After a great UEFA Cup campaign in his first season, only being eliminated by Parma, Advocaat's team was unlucky, twice, not to qualify for the knock-out stages of the Champions League. During those campaigns the side achieved great wins away from home against the likes of PSV and Monaco while the best home results came against Sturm Graz and PSV again. In both seasons, one goal would have seen the team progress in the Champions League, but it was not to be.

After the double season, the future looked bright, the future looked oranji – and then Martin O' Neill joined Celtic and turned things around there instantly. While Celtic were winning the treble in his first season, Advocaat's Rangers were beginning to struggle. This barren season, followed by being well-adrift of Celtic in the table halfway through the next season, resulted in Advocaat being appointed director of football to be replaced in the manager's position by Hibs' boss Alex McLeish, who at least salvaged the second half of that season by winning both domestic Cups, beating Celtic in each.

## MANAGER: DICK ADVOCAAT (1998–2001)

Following the previous trophyless season, few fans could have envisaged Rangers winning yet another treble in the 1998–99 season, especially under the management of a new boss and Gers' first foreign manager. The former Holland coach and PSV Eindhoven manager had had months to examine his new club's players before arriving on the scene. Most of the old guard had been allowed to leave, and virtually a new side had to be assembled by the Dutchman. Luckily for him, David Murray provided the necessary funds to achieve this. By the end of his first season, Advocaat would have spent £30 million on his team that would win everything domestically and show improved performances in the UEFA Cup. Just as important, his teams would always try to play skilful, exciting, attacking football that at times was a joy to behold.

'The Little General', as Advocaat became known, was a strict disciplinarian, and he made sure that the players knew who was boss from the start. A system of fines was put into effect so that even turning up a minute late for lunch was penalised. Advocaat may have been a modern European coach with new methods of training and tactical ploys, but in one sense he was very much in the Rangers tradition. He insisted on his players being well-dressed and projecting a smart image on and off the field. Despite his strict attention to time-keeping, appearance and discipline, however, Advocaat did have a sense of humour that he probably used more on members of the press than his players. It took many of his players quite a while to work out how far they could go with him in terms of banter, but eventually they realised the boundaries.

As stated above, Advocaat assembled a veritable United Nations of players for his new club. The big question was would they be united on the park? As might have been expected over the coming seasons, Advocaat seemed to rely on his Dutch contingent that eventually swelled to number Numan, van Bronckhorst, Mols, de Boer, Ricksen and Konterman. Gers fans sometimes wondered if the Dutch had formed a clique within the dressing room, but while trophies were being won it did not seem to matter, if that were the case.

In Advocaat's first season the only real mishap came in November when the side, reduced to 10 men in the first half, lost 5–1 to Celtic at Celtic Park. By now, nobody could have doubted that Advocaat was an attacking manager, and the downside of this could be seen in this match. Playing with only 10 men from early in the first half, Rangers had gone 3–0 down but had kept attacking. By half-time a goal had been pulled back, but the side was still in danger of being thrashed. Most previous managers would have recognised the reality of the situation and perhaps reorganised the team in a more cautious way in order to minimise the eventual deficit. Not Advocaat though. It was as if he still thought that Rangers could salvage something from the match.

The final score humiliated Rangers fans and some of the die-hard players like Ian Ferguson who were still at Ibrox. Many fans wondered if the foreigners really understood what such a result meant to the Gers fans; however, no real damage was done. A week later, at the same venue, Rangers won the League Cup by beating St Johnstone. As the season progressed, the manager added to his squad signing stars such as Stefan Klos from Borussia Dortmund, French striker, Stephane Guivarc'h from Newcastle, Claudio Reyna from Wolfsburg and Neil McCann from Hearts. Also, in a thrilling climax to the season, Advocaat's side got sweet revenge over Celtic by clinching the Championship when beating Celtic 3–0 at Celtic Park. Not content with that, a one-goal win over Celtic saw the Scottish Cup won and the treble achieved in his first season. A new revolution, the Advocaat revolution, looked as if it had started a new era at Ibrox.

Things continued in much the same vein in Advocaat's second season and, but for an undeserved League Cup defeat of an under-strength Gers side at Pittodrie, the treble might have been repeated. Instead, Advocaat had to make do with the double, gaining revenge over the Dons by thrashing them 4–0 in the Scottish Cup Final in May. Progress in Europe, after reaching the UEFA Cup third round the previous season, continued in the Champions League. Wins home and away against his former club PSV Eindhoven and a draw against Bayern at Ibrox had set Rangers up to qualify for the next group stage – if they could hold Bayern to a draw in Munich in the final match. In one of Rangers' best, but unluckiest, performances in Europe, a penalty goal saw Bayern go through, despite Rangers being the better side and hitting the woodwork more than once. An even bigger blow was the terrible knee injury to star striker Michael Mols, who was out for the rest of the season and never quite the same player again.

In fact, Advocaat was never quite the same manager again either. Few realised it at the time, but Rangers had by now seen the best of Dick Advocaat. In his third season, he faced the challenge of a new Celtic manager in Martin O'Neill and the first Old Firm game of the season should have set alarm bells ringing when Celtic, playing at home, won the match 6–2. Despite the fact that Rangers won the next Old Firm game at Ibrox 5–1, it was obvious that the side was struggling to keep pace with this new Celtic team. Even the purchase of Ronald de Boer from Barcelona and players such as Ricksen, Konterman, Miller, Lovenkrands, Johnston and Ritchie had not improved the side as devastating, long-term injuries took their toll. Also, halfway through the season the acquisition of gangling Norwegian striker Tore Andre Flo from Chelsea for a record £12 million could not turn the team around before the end of the season in which Celtic swept the boards.

In Europe it was disappointment again after things had looked more promising than ever. After having thrashed Austrians Sturm Graz 5–0 at Ibrox and beaten Monaco away, a defeat and draw against Galatasaray plus defeat in Austria meant that Rangers had to beat Monaco at Ibrox in the final game to progress. Leading 2–1, in control, with only 12 minutes left, a silly goal was conceded and a third goal just would not come Rangers' way, thus propelling the team into the UEFA Cup as a consolation. It was after this disappointment that Advocaat rather brutally stripped Lorenzo Amoruso of the captaincy and awarded it to young Barry Ferguson who, despite the doubters, made a success of it.

So, as Advocaat entered his fourth season in charge, he must have known that it was imperative that the initiative be seized back from Celtic. Unfortunately, despite further additions to his playing staff, the team still trailed Celtic in the League by a long way before the season had even reached its halfway point. Everybody at Ibrox realised by then that the title could not be regained that season. In football circles, the talk was that the manager had 'lost the dressing room' and that he might not survive another disastrous season. But before such speculation could gain serious momentum, Dick Advocaat surprised everybody once again by voluntarily changing his position in the club. At the start of December 2001 he became the club's first director of football and was instrumental in Alex McLeish, the Hibs manager, being appointed to the Ibrox hot seat. Within a year, however, Advocaat had left the club altogether to become the coach, once again, of the Dutch national team. His revolution had been short-lived but very, very interesting.

Dick Advocaat won two League Championships, two Scottish Cups and two League Cups.

# *Players Elected*

## Stefan Klos (1998–2007)

When Dick Advocaat became the Rangers manager, one of his priorities was to find a goalkeeper to replace 'The Goalie', Andy Goram, who had been allowed to leave the club in the summer of 1998. His first attempt saw him buy the third-choice 'keeper of that year's French World Cup-winning squad – Lionel Charbonnier from Auxerre. Initially the Frenchman was a hit with the fans and the manager, although his brilliance at times could be erratic. Thus rumours came about that Advocaat was trying to bring German 'keeper Stefan Klos to the club as a replacement. This became a more urgent requirement when Charbonnier was injured playing in a UEFA Cup match against Bayer Leverkusen. Finnish 'keeper Antti Niemi was used as a stopgap, but it was obvious that he did not enjoy his manager's confidence.

Advocaat persevered in his attempt at prising Klos away from Borussia Dortmund, where he was in the final year of his contract. He had already told his club that he wanted to leave so it became a case of when and for how much? On Christmas Eve 1998 Advocaat's persistence paid off when the German signed for a fee of £700,000. He was going to be the third 'keeper that season to try and exorcise the ghost of Andy Goram. If any 'keeper could do it, then it had to be Klos. He had already won the Champions League with Dortmund when they had defeated Juventus in the 1997 Final, and he had played at Ibrox when his team had come up against Rangers in the same tournament in the 1994–95 season, so Rangers were getting an experienced campaigner.

Like Goram, Klos was relatively small for a 'keeper, being 5ft 10in tall. Other similarities were that he tended to be a goalline 'keeper, only coming out for crosses when absolutely necessary and, even then, preferring to punch the ball rather than try to catch it. Also like 'The Goalie', he was a great shot-stopper thanks to very quick reflexes, and he was a master at staying on his feet for as long as possible when a forward burst through to be one-on-one with him, forcing the striker to decide how to get the ball beyond the 'keeper. Unlike Goram, however, he was not as comfortable with the ball at his feet or when it came to dealing with pass-backs. His kicking was also markedly inferior to Goram's. All those weaknesses, though, were overshadowed by the brilliance of his saves, his cool temperament and fierce concentration that made him an absolute star with the Rangers fans in spite of his unassuming personality.

From his first season at the club, fans of all teams in Scotland acknowledged Klos as the finest 'keeper in the country. Like all great 'keepers, he quietly went about his business, making saves at vital points in matches that ultimately made sure of the points or progress into another round of a Cup. Another similarity he shared with Andy Goram was the way he seemed to relish appearing in Old Firm matches and performing at his best. In latter seasons, when perhaps Celtic had the best of most Old Firm encounters, many a time it was the saves of Klos that kept Rangers in the game or, at worst, reduced the margin of defeat – something Gers fans were grateful for.

Klos' wonderful saves are too numerous to detail but perhaps a description of one might be enough to prove the 'keeper's value to Rangers. In the 2002–03 season, with Gers neck-and-neck with Celtic for the title, it had all come down to the final match of the League season. Rangers faced Dunfermline at Ibrox, while Celtic played at Kilmarnock. In the second half, with Gers leading 3–1, Klos pulled off a magnificent save to prevent a 20-yard screamer going into the Rangers net. If that had gone in, it is possible that Celtic would have taken the title by one goal instead of Rangers. He was the unsung hero that day but is recognised as a true hero nowadays. He was an ever present in that treble-winning season.

Further proof of his status can be seen in the fact that Alex McLeish made Klos the new Rangers captain following the departure of Craig Moore and the nickname that the adoring Gers fans saw fit to award him: 'Der Goalie' – no greater tribute could have been made to a worthy successor to the legend that is Andy Goram.

Halfway through the 2004–05 season, in January, a serious training ground injury that resulted in cruciate ligament damage cost him his place, and McLeish signed Ronald Waterreus, the experienced former Dutch international 'keeper. When Klos was fit for the start of the next season, however, his manager decided that Waterreus should retain the 'keeper's jersey, and Klos only made two appearances that season before getting injured again in a cycling accident during the close season. New manager Paul Le Guen brought in French 'keeper Lionel Letizi when Waterreus moved on that summer, leaving Klos as the Gers' number-three 'keeper in effect, behind youngster Alan McGregor who would soon become the number one at the club. Der Goalie decided to retire at the end of that season after making his final bow on the pitch at the end of the last League match at Ibrox, sharing the adulation with another Ibrox hero, Dado Prso. He retired to his home in Switzerland, maybe the best place not to go cycling.

Stefan Klos played 264 games for Rangers. He won four League Championships, four Scottish Cups and two League Cups.

ND - #0263 - 270225 - C0 - 234/156/15 - PB - 9781780913919 - Gloss Lamination